Dedication

I dedicate this book to my wonderful wife Patricia; our three wonderful
children Brian, Mike and Katie; and our friendly friends—Ben our always
very happy dog, who recently became an Angel, and
Buddy, our always cheerful Catholic cat.

Thank You All!

The Candidate's Bible

How to organize and run a successful campaign for public office.

Why on earth should anybody get involved in politics? An untested neophyte would answer: "What's not to love?" The political lifestyle seems enjoyable. There are lots of parties, great seats at events, and of course just like Cheers, everyone knows you name? Let me say it again: "What's not to love?" Yet, when a prospective candidate looks at the reality of the game, however, the more experienced person will say that the political life is a difficult life— far more difficult than it seems at first blush.

Political candidates are continually forced to run through hoops. They are sliced and diced every way possible, especially when their chances of winning are good. Everybody wants a piece of them including the media and their ultimate constituents. Their tax returns are made public . Both old friends and old enemies are interviewed by an unfriendly media, and the candidate's every word is checked for mistakes and gaffes—the more the better.

The bottom line is that it's grueling, tiring, busy, and difficult. There is always something to do. There is always someone who wants something from you. and did I say you are always tired. Yet, somehow, you have to walk around with a smile on your face and a nice comment ready to come from your lips even if it is a bad day. Even if your purpose for running is altruistic so you can help your city, state, or the country, and you really do not want to be a politician, just a worthy representative of the people, there are many who simply will not believe you.

The political game itself is rigged. You need way too much money to win. Regular folks like me for example who run for office have only enough money to live so shortcuts always must be taken to achieve any political gains on a poor man's budget. One such way is to be a write-in candidate, and another is to have a pack of friends willing to work hard for signatures on ballot petitions and to help arrange speaking engagements and public places where you can drop in to greet the folks.

Though you are not a fool, many will call your quest a fool's errand. Try running for office in a state such as Pennsylvania, in which the political incumbents and the establishment have the game 100% rigged. Corrupt state politicians in all 50 states have slanted the ballot-access table in favor of incumbents and against non-political regular citizens of America such as me and you when you become inclined to throw your hat in the ring. The alternative of course is not attractive. If not you, then who—a dirty rotten politician, and we just cannot have that.

Using this experience as a basis, this book is written to help all potential candidates understand the reality of restrictive ballot access laws in all the states and what one must do to comply with them and/or get around them. It presents a program that can be used to help you win election to public office. When you choose to run, it will serve as an effective learning tool and a how-to guide. It contains a lot of great platform information, a great announcement speech, and helpful stuff that you can use in your campaign.
You won't want to put this book down as you learn the ins & outs of running for office and the rudiments of running a campaign. Moreover, you will gain insights about how I ran on the ballot for Congress in 2010, a write-in for the US Senate in 2012, Mayor in 2015, and now again in 2018 as a write-in candidate for the US Senate.

I freely admit that I have yet to win an election, but I now know what it would take to win. Besides being able to raise money, which is the ugliest part of running for office, to win an election you must have the heart of Robert the Bruce (think spider) and the spirit of *The Little Engine That Could,* and you have to be willing to lose a few times before you finally win.

ii

Copyright © August 2018, Brian W. Kelly; ....Editor: Brian P. Kelly
Title: The Candidate's Bible   Author Brian W. Kelly
How to organize and run a successful campaign for public office.

Referenced Material: Standard Disclaimer: The information in this book has been obtained through personal and third-party observations, interviews, and copious research. Where unique information has been provided or extracted from other sources, those sources are acknowledged within the text of the book itself or in the References area in the front matter. Thus, there are no formal footnotes nor is there a bibliography section. Any picture that does not have a source was taken from various sites on the Internet with no credit attached. If resource owners would like credit in the next printing, please email publisher.

Published by: .... LETS GO PUBLISH!
Editor in Chief...Brian P. Kelly
Email: .... info@letsgopublish.com
Web site..www.letsgopublish.com

Library of Congress Copyright Information Pending
Book Cover Design by **Brian W. Kelly**

Text Editor—Brian P. Kelly

ISBN Information: The International Standard Book Number (ISBN) is a unique machine-readable identification number, which marks any book unmistakably. The ISBN is the clear standard in the book industry. 159 countries and territories are officially ISBN members. The Official ISBN for this book is

978-1-947402-49-2

The price for this work is:................ .... **$ 9.95 USD**

10	9	8	7	6	5	4	3	2	1

Release Date: .... August 2018

LETS GO PUBLISH!

Acknowledgments

I appreciate all the help that I have received in putting this book together as well as all of my other 164 other published books.

My printed acknowledgments had become so large that book readers "complained" about going through too many pages to get to page one of the text.

And, so to permit me more flexibility, I put my acknowledgment list online, and it continues to grow. Believe it or not, it once cost about a dollar more to print each book.

Thank you and God bless you all for your help.

Please check out www.letsgopublish.com to read the latest version of my heartfelt acknowledgments updated for this book. FYI, Wily Ky Eyely, my wonderful basketball playing "niece," loves this book and recommends it to all. She wants "Uncle Brian" to be our next US Senator.

Click the bottom of the Main menu to see the big acknowledgments!

Thank you all!

Preface

Why did Brian W. Kelly write this book?

Brian W. Kelly loves America and he developed a number of unique approaches to solving some problems in America, from which Pennsylvanians suffer about as much as those from other states. Four times Brian Kelly has run for public office. Twice he went through the ballot access process as he ran for Congress in Northeastern PA and he ran for Mayor in his home town of Wilkes-Barre, PA.

On another two times, Kelly ran for the US Senate as a write-in candidate as the cost in time and money for a regular person to achieve 2000 nomination petition signatures and travel around the state of Pennsylvania was far too prohibitive. Sometimes getting one's platform exposed to the public is reward enough when the full goal is unachievable.

Brian Kelly gets much of his message out in the books he writes. This book is Brian's 166th of 166 books in total. A number of his books are on topics such as high tech and sports while others are about important issues such as illegal immigration. Each of the immigration books, written in different time periods, either further define the problem or refine the solution to illegal immigration and the millions of foreign interlopers in America today. Kelly's solution revealed in his platform for Americans solves the problem once and for all of upwards of 60 million illegal foreign residents living in the shadows.

He provides his 2018 Senate announcement speech in this book for you to use as a basis for any of your own speeches that you may choose to write and deliver to your constituents.

Brian wrote this book to be your candidate's bible among other reasons because he cares about Pennsylvania and America. I am publishing this book because I care. In this document, Kelly identifies what you will need to do to get your campaign going and he offers many tips for structuring and sequencing events as you move from announcement day to election days.

I am sure you will construct your own platform similarly, based on the information Brian provides as examples, and that your unique solutions for seniors, millennials, and the rest of us will aid in your success on the campaign trail. When elected for public office, of course you will work hard to assure your platform points become reality. Your constituents will ask you why "nobody else ever thought of that," when you put your platform points together and you roll out your campaign. .

I hope you enjoy this book and I hope that it inspires you to take the individual actions necessary to help the government of the US stand firm against any attacks on democracy from outside or from within this great country.

Brian W. Kelly has the solutions to help a dedicated American achieve success as a political candidate—even a candidate that may not interested in ever being a "politician."

I wish you the best.

Brian P. Kelly, Publisher
Wilkes-Barre, Pennsylvania

Table of Contents

About the Author

Brian W. Kelly retired as an Assistant Professor in the Business Information Technology (BIT) program at Marywood University, where he also served as the IBM i and Midrange Systems Technical Advisor to the IT Faculty. Kelly designed, developed, and taught many college and professional courses. He continues as a contributing technical editor to a number of IT industry magazines, including "The Four Hundred" and "Four Hundred Guru," published by IT Jungle.

Kelly is a former IBM Senior Systems Engineer and IBM Mid Atlantic Area Specialist. His specialty was designing applications for customers as well as implementing advanced IBM operating systems and software facilities on their machines.

He has an active information technology consultancy. He is the author of 171 books and numerous technical articles. Kelly has been a frequent speaker at COMMON, IBM conferences, and other technical conferences.

Brian was a candidate for US Congress from Pennsylvania in 2010 and he brings a lot of experience to his writing endeavors. Brian is ready to be your Senator in 2019.

Chapter 1 Factors to Examine Before Running for Office

Should I run for office?

In order to answer that, please let me tell you what made me think I ever could run for office. It was not something I had ever wanted; and it was never something I thought I could achieve if I wanted it. I ran a private business called Kelly Consulting, an information technology consulting firm, specializing in IBM midrange computer systems such as the AS/400 at the time.

One of my tech consulting accounts at the time , Klein Wholesale Candy kept me busy on many projects. One day I showed up in the IT Director's office for a discussion and he had his team primed for my arrival but not on a project topic. There were four programmer analysts close-by in four desks on one side of the room while in the middle of the room was the Director's desk facing theirs. He had a number of PCs and servers scattered behind him and on the side of his area. It was the company's software development room where they kept the business up to date by creating and modifying programs. The big systems that I kept up-to-date for the team were on the other side of the building.

As I took my seat in front of the Director's desk, they started. It was well rehearsed. One after another. First one voice, then another, and then another. The Director, a fine fellow named Dennis Grimes, finally admitted that together they had decided that they were going to do what they needed to do to nominate me to run for Congress and I should not try to talk them out of it. I was speechless.

However, the more I thought about the idea it in the next several minutes, the more I liked it and the more they knew I liked it, the more inclined they were to let me know that they were just busting me. They were not at all serious.

The thought never left me after that day and when I got home, that was probably the first time that I ever talked to my wife about running for any public office. She was glad they were only kidding but now I was really tuned in to the possibility of becoming a Congressman. What not? I thought! Right! Why not?

After three tries, in 2018, I am going after the prize one more time. But this time unlike my first time, I do not expect to win, and I will not spend anything but the government fees that are required. Win or lose, I do want to influence the prevailing thinking on several points that I raise in my announcement speech which is presented in Chapter 13.

Should you run for office?

Now we are talking. Yes, you should! Absolutely, yes!

If you are thinking of running for office but maybe not for five or ten years, you can begin a lot of this stuff right now and go through a few practice runs . For example, why not run for office as a write-in candidate? It costs just about nothing and you will get to think about a lot of things. Another thought is to run for Mayor or Council or something that needs just ten to 100 signatures on a petition. Be careful as you may win. Don't get too caught up in expenses if this is just a test because, let me repeat: You may win. Then what?

Before taking your next step towards becoming the desired *so and so from such and such*, a prospective candidate must do a lot of thinking. Mom, dad, sister Susie, the neighbors, and the guys on the softball team can all help put the notion in perspective, but they cannot answer that question. It is your decision and you cannot take it lightly. Only you can answer whether you are going to give it a go. Are you willing to work that hard to win and afterwards, to serve?

The factors you should examine are many but # 1 on the list would be your relationship with your family and the level of support if any that you can expect from them. It all matters.

Years before I finally decided to run for Congress for example (I ran in in 2010), I spoke with my wife about it. I don't want to say that she shuddered at the thought; but it did not make her happy. My life, my three kids, and my dear wife were and still are much more important than running for any office no matter how much of a calling I may have thought I had.

And, so, several times before we agreed that I could run for office, I decided not to run. It was definitely years of light discussion When I finally decided to run, it was the right time. The moon was in the seventh house and Jupiter was aligned with Mars and peace was guiding the planets and love was steering the stars. It was the dawning of the age of Aquarius. As an Aquarian myself, born on January 30, it was my time to see and help if I could, the peace, by taking part of the helm in directing the US to be more in synch with the people.

I was ready; but I still did not have enough money to run with any assurance of victory. But, I wanted to see. I had a few thousand dollars for yard signs and a few newspaper ads and incidentals such as the $200 fee to get on the ballot, and the $200 to get all of the nomination petitions notarized.

Because it was my first time ever running for anything other than student council, I used my perception of the America that I knew to guide me in my campaign decisions. So, I decided that I would not take any donations. I did not think the founders intended neighbors to chip in money – just the time to take care of the farm after asking one of their own to represent them.

I did not want to take a dollar from anybody, friend or foe, and decided that I would minimize my own expenditures as I would still have to go to work to feed the family after the election—or so I surmised.

In this process, I learned that one cannot win an election with no money. However, one can set the stage for the next election and the next by being on the ballot without spending a lot of money. I got 17% of the vote in my first try. The pundits in my home town who had not endorsed me were amazed at the voting percentage that I had achieved. At my small gathering when they counted the ballots, the first town in was White Haven, one of the few places that gave me space for a speech. I won in White Haven and let me tell you all, it was a glorious feeling.

Like me, I would recommend that you Sit down with your spouse and children to discuss your idea of running for office. Do your best to explain the job and your reasons for wanting the job to be sure that they're "on board" with your decision to run. Preferably, it should be a decision that your family makes together.

Of course, if you are head strung, you can run without your family's support, but I would not advise it. Campaigns take a toll on the candidate, as well as on the spouse and the children. No matter how much fun it seems to be from casual observance, the hours are long and irregular, and the pace is exhausting. Take it from me. You need solid family support behind you.

Campaigns are demanding and often require you're putting the rest of your life "on hold" for several months. You will surely miss some family events, not being around as much. You must make sure your family understands and is o.k. with this scenario.

Having said that, if you do run for office, be sure to continue making time for your family. Show up at the basketball and soccer events as well as the recitals and concerts, bring your family along on campaign stops and to "political" events. I think they will enjoy being there and they will be proud of you for doing what you are doing to help out.

There is no question that you will have to work hard. So, are you willing to work hard?

Even though it may not appear so when you take the first step, running for office is hard work. Ask yourself a lot of times: "Are you ready for it?" Depending on the position you are seeking, running for office may mean twelve-hour days for months, with only one or two days off. It may mean making calls to potential supporters for five straight hours, taking a short lunch, then doing it all over again. It will definitely mean getting verbally attacked by your opponent, and quite possible by the media or other stakeholders. Can you handle it?

Be sure, before you throw your hat in the ring, that you're ready to work harder than you ever have in your life and be emotionally spent by the end of every day, without getting mad, and remembering the reasons why you got into politics in the first place.

The answer is "Yes you can" when your question is "Can I do it?"

Here is another tough question. Do you think you can collect money for your campaign, so you can buy things you need such as yard signs, magnetic signs for your car, etc.? Do you think that you have it in you to ask someone for $100 or $500 or $1000 and still maintain a straight face? If you're like me, that will be your toughest job unless you are using this run as a trial run and the real campaign will be several years out.

Nobody likes to raise money. But as a candidate, you will have to raise money. It is expected and let me repeat that: As a candidate, you will have to raise money... yourself and with others.

Do not be like the guy who always loses and is not OK with it. Many in your position come into the political process thinking that, if they just have some good ideas and stick to working on the issues most important to the office. The others on the team will go out and raise the money for them. It will not happen

The "dirty little secret" of politics is that if you're not willing to go out and raise money for yourself, nobody will be out there to raise funds for you. There are other secrets, but they tell me that the next best secret is that nobody in your campaign will be a better fund raiser than you. Those who make contributions are not necessarily interested in making them to your friends on the baseball team or your brother. They want to make their contributions to the candidate, not to a staff member or supporter. It's that simple.

I am not suggesting that you will have to raise all (or even most) of the money on your own. Very few, if any, candidates have enough personal contacts to raise $1 million, $10 million, or $50 million on their own. Don't get scared by the numbers. Remember, once you do a few of the trial runs we discussed, you will get good at it.

Most of us couldn't even raise $50,000 on our own on our best day, especially if all we had was our personal contacts list. Don't worry, if they see you leading, they will absolutely help, and you can use tactics like direct mail, events, etc. to raise money without doing it face-to-face.

To get better at fundraising, there are a lot of sites available on the Internet such as

http://www.localvictory.com/category/fundraising

The key thing is that it is you who will have to raise money for your campaign, and most of the early money will come from your own fundraising efforts, and some from your own pocket if you can afford it. The following is from the above web site.

You Have to Believe in the Process!

The biggest questions of our day... the really important ones, like healthcare, abortion, civil rights, war and peace... they are all decided in the political sphere. From local town governments to the White House, politicians and their staffs decide on matters great and small that affect the lives of everyone on Earth. Whether you believe in big government or small, natural law or positivism, free markets or regulation, get involved in government for the right reason: because you want to have an impact on those important decisions, for the good of your fellow man.

Don't let anyone tell you, when you're running for office, that you're getting into a "dirty" profession. Sure, there have been many political scoundrels over the course of human history. Sure, many people believe that the best government is the smallest government. But the practice of politics has a long and storied history and has made a great amount of good possible throughout time.

If someone tells you that all of politics is a dirty affair, remind them that George Washington, William Wilberforce, Ghandi, Teddy Roosevelt, Edmund Burke and countless other statesmen and women have been involved and engaged in the political process.

If You're Running, Run to Win!

Whether you're jumping into politics for the first time, or trying to move up to a higher office, make sure that you're in it to win. There's no point running if you're not running to win. It's hard work, and some days you're not going to feel like getting up and shaking hands or making phone calls. Other days, when the polls show you behind, you'll wonder whether you really should have run in the first place.

Don't second guess your decision. Once you're in the race, unless some truly unique circumstance presents itself that prevents you from continuing, keep chugging along. Work hard. Make the calls. Shake the hands. And use the knowledge and information you learn on Local Victory to do your very best to win your election.

You can do it!

Chapter 2 When You Decide; Start Reading

BE THE CHANGE!

★ RUN FOR OFFICE ★

In making the decision to run

There are lots of how to's and to do's when one finally decides to run for public office at any level. There are official and unofficial documents that can help in making the decision. They also aid in helping the prospective candidate know what to do. All the write-ups by well-meaning government entities are written in a way to sweeten up the candidate's idea of running for office so that they will choose to run.

These are not bad sites. They do not tell prospects for candidacy not to run for office because "your friends will think you are a jerk." But, they might as well say that. Just like my friends, your friends will question your motivation and they will question your ability to beat machine politics in any state.

For Pennsylvanians considering the plunge, there is a wonderful fact-filled write-up that appears to have been written by the state. It is hosted by Wyoming County, PA. You can get to it online through your web browser by typing in *wycopa running for public office*. The actual URL web address is complicated so use this search argument in a search engine and it will better help you access the document.

Much of what I present in these next few chapters is based on this document plus I throw in my personal experience as I also do throughout the chapters in the book. I went through the whole process as a neophyte in 2010 when I ran for Congress, once again in 2012, as I ran as a write-in for the US Senate, and once in 2015 as I ran for Mayor of Wilkes-Barre, PA.

You might say that I have had my fill of such instructions and following them to the letter of the law. But, I am at it again running for the US Senate in 2018 as a write-in candidate. I will talk about write-in options later in the various essays throughout the book.

When I ran for Congress in 2010, I got 17% of the vote and five years later in my home town, I got just 5% of the vote when I ran for Mayor. I also spent more money in 2015. I have learned many lessons. My net gain from all this activity is that I now get to say that I ran for office. Additionally, I know what I would need to do to win when and if that becomes my objective.

I am glad that I did all that and I am running again but as a write-in, I will no longer have to spend large sums of money to get on the ballot and conduct any campaign and get my message out. I run for office hoping to help the City / State / Country in which I live handle the pressures of today more effectively. I know that I would do better than politicians—the likes of which we wind up electing time and time again.

A side desire of mine has always been to get rid of the machine from controlling government at all levels to help bring the government back to the people. So far, I have been unsuccessful because the system is definitely rigged. Yet, I continue to have hope that somebody will emerge to take on the bad guys and bring the people a victory. I hope it is you.

Maybe one day it will be me. Maybe it will be you. So far, it looks like our best hope is to find more people in the country like Donald Trump. Like him or not, we all have to believe that Donald Trump is an impressive man.

It surely does not have to be me. I hope it is you. I would love for everybody who once thought about running for office and hopefully is thinking about doing so again, to promise they will never vote for another two-term incumbent. That is a first step in making the process fair. The people have to get rid of the existing bad guys or as many like to say, "Throw the bums out!" It can become a fair system but not without help from the people at election time. It won't change until we throw out the people that made it like it is.

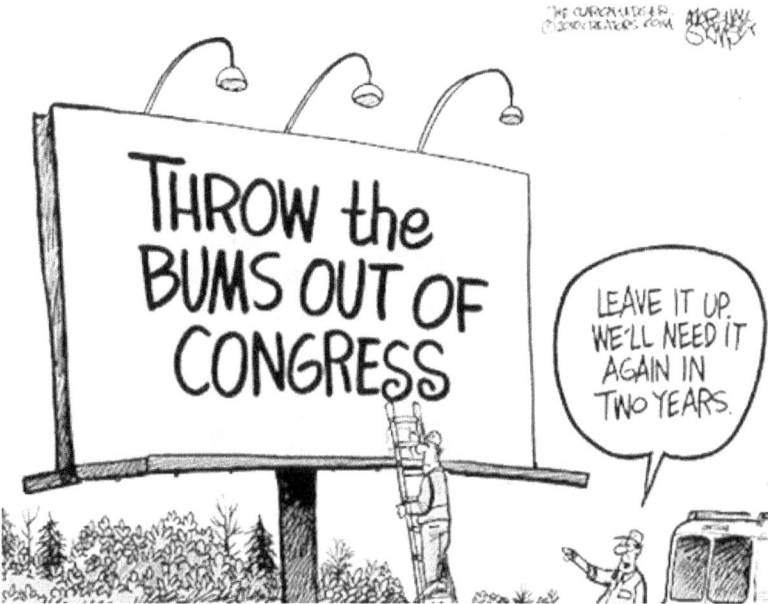

Government, my friends is bad because we have elected scoundrels to offices that are important for all the people. Additionally, a SWAMP of officials from after many years of service to government, though employees, begin to operate on their own for political reasons. Good personnel systems and people who vote are needed to get rid of them.

The people we have elected in many if not most cases have become greedy and self-centered. They have distanced themselves from the needs of their constituents and the people they swear to serve.

One of the most important things that a prospective candidate for office must do is a self-evaluation. You must be sure that you are ready both for the possibility of success and the probability of many disappointments along the way.

Unfortunately, a prospective candidate for public office using traditional methods also needs to determine if he or she can afford the commitment of time, money and energy necessary to run for the intended office.

Though the official documents make it seem like it is 1, 2, 3, the fact is the incumbents have made the process unnecessarily difficult. Therefore many, once engaged, begin to think that they cannot really run for office. Expect obstacles and you will not be disappointed.

Let's suppose for a minute that you are certified Mensa (The High IQ Society), but you have minimal resources and even less cash. You are going to have a tough time without donors.

To be successful using the traditional approach of getting on the ballot is very difficult without a pile of money. In my case, running for Congress, I had to buy a lot of yard signs and other material to help myself become known. It cost me about $5000.00 in 2010 and I took no donations to remain free of political encumbrances and entanglements. I wanted nobody to own me. In retrospect, I was too strict as family donating $50 or $100 each would not create an issue.

In addition to money, a prospective candidate must also make sure that he or she is qualified to hold the office being sought. There are no listed qualifications to make sure this is really true, however. My rule of thumb is that if you think you are qualified, you are. Let the voters decide. Go for it!

Once you have assured all this, and you want to proceed, your next step is very important. You need to check in with your family and friends, especially your immediate family. You must make sure that they are OK with your running for whatever office. In my case it was Congress. I got reluctant acceptance from my immediate family, which told me that it was OK for me to proceed.

You then need a team of good people to help you. You cannot do it alone. The only thing you can do alone in life is fail. You will need people who can think with you and people who can do work for you. There is lots of work from placing signs, creating fliers, speeches, and essays, building a website, and going door to door to get petition signatures.

You also need one very, very good friend, or if you have some money to burn, a good campaigner who will work for you and be paid to organize your campaign. In my case, Marty Devaney, a very good friend of mine understood the system and he worked very effectively with me. He donated his time and effort to the cause. He was my campaign manager and a great man.

Marty and I put together a team of about forty people from my friend and family group. My brothers and sisters were not happy with the idea of my running. So, only a few helped me in the grassroots work. Thankfully, I had a great team of friends and in-laws who were pleased to host a few events and participate as needed as we organized our approach. You'll find that people bring in other people when the benefit to all is better government.

This gave me about three team captains and I could have used more to assure things like signs and nominating petitions were completed. A number for my high school friends asked to help so in the end we had a formidable group. To run for Congress in PA, you need 1000 signatures on your nomination petitions. One of the great measurements of our campaign success was that we got over 1500 signatures in three weeks and less than forty were stricken as invalid.

What should first-time candidates know?

I gave you the search argument for the document you should print and read (*wycopa running for public office*). Pay close attention to the instructions provided and check out all the forms necessary to gain ballot access. Make to-do-lists like I did as you read the documents. See some of my own personal documents at the end of this chapter.

In addition, if you plan to spend more than $5000, or if you have more than $250 in expenses, as a first-time candidate, you need to become familiar with the Campaign Finance Reporting Law, which is posted on the Department of State's website at www.dos.state.pa.us/campaignfinance.

You might want to ask a friend who is an accountant to help you in this regard, even if they charge you as the details on this huge report are tricky. Remember, all of these things are hoops in a gauntlet that you must traverse in order to be deemed qualified to get on the ballot to run for office in PA. Other states have similar restrictions and most have their own twists.

A prospective candidate should also understand the commitment of time and energy necessary to run a successful campaign for public office. No matter what you thought it would be, it will take even more. Why? Because incumbents do not ever want to lose, and they make the rules.

Try getting on the ballot but make sure you are ready to work harder than it ought to be. It is OK to run even if you are not 100% committed. If you lose it will not hurt so much. If you win, you do not have to keep the office forever. In all cases, if you run, you must be prepared to serve the people and enjoy your salary.

Chapter 3 Accessing the Ballot in Your State

What a candidate must file to access the ballot

There is a problem in most states in the union to gain access to the ballot. In 2010, I was the #1 listed candidate for Congress in my district as the Capitol Police in Harrisburg pulled my name first in the position lottery. To be in this ballot position lottery, you must get the required signatures and defend them in Harrisburg or your state capitol.

Signature requirements vary depending on the state in which you reside and the office for which the nomination petition is being circulated. The rule of thumb on nomination signatures is always get twice the number you need.

For example, when I ran for Mayor, I needed 100 signatures. My little team brought in over 250. When I ran for Congress, I needed 1000 signatures. My expanded team brought in over 1500 signatures and we checked them thoroughly to make sure there were no gotchas. We lost only 40 in Harrisburg when they were examined by state officials. Mistakes are inevitable.

To be on the ballot v a write-in, you must inform the state for which office you are running and assure that they send you a campaign packet with the needed forms before the three-week period begins for signature gathering for your nominating petitions. You can get your packet early, but you cannot solicit signatures before the declared first day.

Obviously one of the forms you need is the nomination petition. If the heading information is not filled in properly, an entire petition can be thrown out during the inspection process when you turn them in. In other words, make sure everything is done right or you can lose as many as 50 signatures in one clip.

Below are some forms you will need. They should all be in your packet. To be sure you have the right contacts in the state to get the packet, visit your county election bureau (voter services) and tell them you are running, and they will review what you need. In some cases, depending on the office for which you are seeking, such as Mayor or Council, the County group will have all the forms you need.

For governor or senator or Congress, you will need to get the forms from the state. The county people will tell you how to get them. When you visit the county, ask about getting the CD of voters' names & addresses. This way, you will know who is a Democrat and who is a Republican. If your office spans counties, ask the county voter services head in each county for their CD. When I ran, there was no state-wide CD. They charged me $50.00 at the county level. With 67 counties in PA, this can get expensive.

If you are a Democrat for example, running as a Democrat, you need to get signatures of only Democrats. Republicans get Republican signatures on their petitions. If you are running for a slot on both tickets, you need to get the minimum number for each party to be on their respective ballot ticket in the primary. The form you use for getting signatures is called a nomination petition. Forms are described below:

The Candidates Affidavit
Each candidate must file with his or her nomination petition or nomination paper an affidavit setting forth information about the candidate, including the candidate's residence, election district and the name of the office the candidate is seeking.

The Statement of Financial Interests
The Statement of Financial Interests is a form that must be filed with the State Ethics Commission, which requires the filer to set forth information regarding the filer's sources of income. A copy of the completed Statement of Financial Interests must also accompany the nomination petition of a candidate for state, county or local public

The Nomination Petition
Each page of a nomination petition contains three basic components:

1) the Preamble; 2) the Signatures of Electors; and 3) the Affidavit of Circulator.

The Preamble:
The preamble is the portion of the nomination petition page where information about the candidate is inserted. The preamble includes the office for which the candidate seeks nomination, the name of the candidate, the candidate's occupation, the candidate's residence and the party affiliation of the signers.

Signatures of Electors:
Each person who signs a nomination petition must insert the following information about himself or herself: 1.-Signature; 2.-Printed name; 3.-Address of residence, including street and number, if any; and 4.-The date on which he or she signed the nomination petition

The Affidavit of Circulator:
Each nomination petition page must include the duly executed affidavit of the person who circulated the nomination petition (the circulator). The circulator of the nomination petition page must swear or affirm the following:

That the circulator is a qualified elector of the Commonwealth or of the district, as the case may be.

That the circulator is a duly registered and enrolled member of the political party designated in the nomination petition;
That the circulator's address of residence is as set forth in items 4 and 5 of the affidavit;

That the signers of the nomination petition page signed with the full knowledge of the contents of the nomination petition;

That the signers' residences are correctly stated on the nomination petition page;

That each signer signed on the date that the signer inserted next to his or her signature, name and address of residence; and

That, to the best of the circulator's knowledge and belief the signers are qualified electors, who are duly registered and enrolled in the political party designated in the petitions and are residents in the County set forth in item 1 of the affidavit.

Sorry I had to do that to you in such detail, but it is a game rigged for regular citizens to withdraw rather than proceed.

Please note that unless you are superman, you will need multiple circulators for your petitions. These are the people who ask other people for their signatures. Make sure the circulator information is done correctly above. You may have five circulators and each of them may have various nominating petitions. For example, a circulator may get 50 signatures and then need another petition form. A circulator may choose to keep one at his family residence and in the office and in the car, etc. Each has to be filled out properly. Your opponent would be pleased to find a flaw in your work.

Challenges to Nomination Petitions and Nomination Papers

The system is set up that if John W Public writes John Q Public on the petition for any candidate and it is later proven he is John x Public, his line does not count. If your write an abbreviation for Wilkes-Barre as WB or W-B, that signature or form does not count. Pay attention to the rules. I have a copy of the handout sheet I used for circulators at the end of this chapter.

Entrenched establishment politicians like Joe Sestak or Bob Casey, Jr. will challenge regular guys such as Carl Romanelli or like Joe Vodvarka, hoping to scare them into not running. Typically, an individual such as Sestak can challenge the validity of a nomination petition by a good guy like Vodvarka within seven days of the filing deadline for nomination petitions or nomination papers.

Sestak in 2012 challenged the petitions of Vodvarka because he could not stand the thought of a guy running against him, and he apparently had the resources to squash Vodvarka rather than let him run.

The Candidate List

If you change your mind after you are on the ballot, there is a last day to withdraw or you will be on the ballot regardless. As a valid candidate, you will be asked to come to the state capitol for Congress as an example to draw lots for ballot position. If you do not want to go to Harrisburg for example, the Capitol Police will draw your ballot. I chose the latter method and luck of the Irish, I was listed # 1 on the ballot.

After the last day for candidates who have filed nomination petitions to withdraw and after the candidates have cast lots for position on the primary ballot, the Secretary of the Commonwealth must forward a list of statewide candidates of each party to the various county boards of elections. This is how your county knows you are on the ballot.

A candidate of a minor political party or political body will have his or her name placed on the November ballot upon acceptance of his or her nomination paper by the Department of State or the County Board of Elections, as the case may be, unless the nomination paper is judicially set aside as a result of a successful challenge to the candidate's nomination paper. If you fit in this group, please spend some time talking to some experts to make sure this is done properly. Most of what we have discussed so far is how to get on the Primary ballot.

CAMPAIGN FINANCE REPORTING

Who Must File Campaign Finance Reports/Statements?

Campaign finance reports/statements must be filed by candidates for public office setting forth information regarding contributions received and expenditures made for the purpose of influencing the outcome of an election. A candidate may also authorize a committee to accept contributions and make expenditures on the candidate's behalf. The committee must have a chairperson and a treasurer, who may not be the same person. Each candidate and each authorized political committee must file reports of receipts and expenditures, if the amount received or expended or liabilities incurred exceeds $250. Otherwise, the candidate or the treasurer of the authorized political committee may file the statement in lieu of the reports. Candidates are required to file a campaign finance report/statement that is separate from the report/statement

ELECTION DAY

Electioneering
No person, including a candidate, may electioneer or solicit votes when inside a polling place. All persons, except those persons authorized or be inside the polling place (election officers, clerks, machine inspectors, overseers, watchers, persons in the course of voting, persons lawfully giving assistance to voters, and peace and police officers), must remain at least ten (10) feet from the polling place during the progress of voting.

Watchers
Each candidate may appoint two watchers for each election district (polling place) in which the candidate's name appears on the ballot. However, only one watcher for each candidate may be present in the polling place at any one time.

Candidates interested in appointing watchers should contact the appropriate county board of elections for information about submitting the names of watchers and obtaining certificates for those watchers.

Qualifications of watchers:
Each watcher appointed to serve in an election district must be a registered voter of the county in which the election district is located.

In order to serve as a watcher, a person must receive from the appropriate county board of elections a Watcher's Certificate, which the watcher must present when requested to do so.

Rights of Watchers:
When a watcher is not serving in the election district for which the watcher was appointed, the watcher may serve in any other election district in the county in which the watcher is registered to vote.

Watchers may be present in the polling place from the time the election officers meet prior to the opening of the polls until the time that voting is complete, and the district register and voting check list is locked and sealed, provided that they remain outside the "enclosed space" (the area in which the voting compartments are located).

A watcher is permitted to keep a list of voters and is entitled to challenge the qualifications of a voter in the manner provided by Law. Watchers should take care to issue challenges in good faith. The Pennsylvania Election Code does not authorize wholesale or frivolous challenges, which are intended to intimidate voters

Chapter 4 My Personal Rules for Verifying Signatures

I shortened the big list of stuff that I needed to know and developed and used my own instruction sheet in my 2010 run for Congress. I have made it more appropriate for 2018 in the following pages. These are not state rules. They were my rules and I gave each circulator and anybody part of the team a copy to help avoid mistakes. When I created this "cheat cheat," I made it one sheet.

Look on the www.briankellyforcongress.com web site, the main menu for a pdf of the form called Signature Rules. Picture this on an 8.5 X 11 paper on both sides. Here goes

It is easy for a person who signs your petition to make a mistake. Here is what a cut-out of a nomination petition looks like in PA:

SIGNATURE OF ELECTOR	PRINTED NAME OF ELECTOR	PLACE OF RESIDENCE			DATE OF SIGNING
		House No.	Street or Road	City, Boro or Twp.	
15. Ashley Cintron	Ashley Cintron	1103	Hall St.	Philadelphia	3/2/14
16. Derwin Fullard	Derwin Fullard	1112	Hall St.	Philadelphia	3/2/14
17. Sybil Fulford	Sybil Fulford	112	Hall	Philadelphia	3/2/14
18. Melanie Fullard	Melanie Fullard	112	Hall	Philadelphia	3/2/14
19. Jennifer Johansen	Jennifer Johansen	1118	Hall St.	Philadelphia	3/2/14
20. Gregory Hawkins	Gregory Hawkins	1120	Hall	Philadelphia	3/2/14
21. Lee ann Hawkins	Lee ann Hawkins	120	Hall	Philadelphia	3/2/14
22. Kenneth Blackwell	Kenneth Blackwell	1101	Kimball	Philadelphia	3/2/14
23. Maria Quarles	Maria Quarles	1120	Hall St.	Philadelphia	3/2/14
24. Jeffrey Melton	Jeffrey Melton	1107	Kimball	Philadelphia	3/2/14
25. Susan Cuffie	Susan Cuffie	1109	Kimball	Philadelphia	3/2/14
26. Doreen Cuffie	Doreen Cuffie	1100	Kimball	Philadelphia	3/2/14

Check out the shortened rules that I created on the next page

Rules for Signatures -- Brian Kelly for Congress Page 1

1. Get a clipboard, & Black Pen. -- I should have enough here. Put your stuff in the clipboard

2. Get at least one sheet for each county (Luzerne, Lackawanna, Monroe, Columbia, Carbon) in which you may choose to get signatures -- If your streets are in Luzerne County but Mom and Dads are in Lackawanna County, you need two sheets. Take as many sheets as you think you need (50 signatures max per sheet)

3. Look at the sheet. Note that Item 6 is the County. Luzerne is filled in on some sheets. If you go to counties outside of Luzerne, before getting any signatures fill in the County Name. Do not mix people from different counties on the same form.

4. Look at the sheet. Each sheet holds 50 signatures. You are to observe the person filling out the signature line. Use just one line each to sign and complete their line on the petition.

5. Look at the sheet. The top of the sheet page 1 is already filled out other than county in some cases. [I did this when I copied the forms for Luzerne County where most of my circulators were] The note to the Secretary of the Commonwealth is next. This describes what the signature / line is all about. It is not a vote. It is your agreement that a fellow citizen (me) in the 17th district may run for Congress.

6. Look at the sheet. Lines 1 to 29 and heading. Space for 29 signatures on Page 1.

7. Look at the sheet. In the signature space, this is how the signature and other information is to be printed / signed. Ditto marks are not permitted anywhere.

A. **SIGNATURE OF ELECTOR** -- Each signer of the nominating petition is an elector -- i.e. one who has a right to vote D (Democrat) in the primary and is in District 17. (If your case is Republican, make sure the signer is Republican – do not mix Ds and Rs on same sheet) Observe the signatory sign in that space. The signature itself must be in cursive form - not printed.

B. **PRINTED NAME of ELECTOR** -- Caution the signatory that the name in the signature and the name printed are the same name - initials or no initials etc. Observe the signatory print their name the same as on their official records -- such as driver's license. Use middle initial if on license.

C. **PLACE OF RESIDENCE - HOUSE #-** Observe just house # printed in this space.

D. **PLACE OF RESIDENCE - Street or Rd**. Caution the signatory to place the street or road with the designator St. Rd. or Ave. followed by apartment # (apt 1) if there is such a #. Observe the signatory type this information. Street, road, or avenue may be abbreviated but not the street name.

E. **PLACE OF RESIDENCE - City, Boro, or Twp**. Caution the signatory to use no abbreviations for the municipality. For example WB, W.B., W-B, W-Barre are all invalid and will cause the signature to be thrown out.

F. **Date of SIGNING**. Observe the signatory print the date while cautioning that it must be correct and within the period of February 16 to March 9, 2010 (check the dates).

For example, 02/16/2010 is valid and 02/16/2009 is not. Any date such as 02/15/2010 or before this date is not valid. Any date such as 03/10/2010 or after this date is not valid.

Any mistakes on date will cause the signature to be thrown out.

Circulators should make sure that the dates on the form are oldest to newest sequence. March 8 should not be before March 1 on the form. Examples below use a random date.

AA. Note on the signature line --- >> If the signatory makes a number of mistakes and it does not look good. It will not be accepted. Draw a straight line through the whole line and ask them to start over on the next line. Do not waste lines.

BB. Lines 30 to 50 are valid spaces for signatures -- thus each sheet can hold a maximum of 50 signatures (29 on front and 21 on back). Get as many forms as you need!

CC. Each Saturday beginning February 20 (pick date), please call D. Greemez with the # of signatures that you obtained that week.

The sooner we get all the forms to Harrisburg the better. 655-5555. Or email <greemez@comcast.net>

DD. On February 27 or March 6, depending on how we are doing, all forms need to be brought to BK's house (candidate) and we will have them notarized. We will have a notary onsite to do this. He or she will do them all at once and charge BK, not the circulator. Circulators must be present to sign in front of Notary

EE. On March 2 or March 9 BK will take the notarized forms to Harrisburg. If you cannot come to get the forms notarized, please have them notarized in your area and BK will reimburse you the expense. BK will come to your house to pick up the notarized form, hopefully before March 2.

FF. Look at the form on the back in the affidavit of circulator. You are the circulator. Do not fill this out the left side at all and do not fill in the right side until all the signatures are on the sheet and the Notary Public is standing in front of you.

GG. Make sure Brian gets as many forms as possible filled with signatures and that they are notarized either at the meeting on Feb 27 or March 6 or by you and your own Notary.

HH. Some have asked for data sheets. Get your data sheets now! Tell Brian what streets / towns you want if your sheets are not ready. Verify that the person signing actually signs their name as it is listed in the data sheet or their Driver's License (should be the same)

II. Can you get anybody's signature? Yes, they know if they have previously signed for Brian so don't worry about it. Get the signature - Democrat -- District 17. Make sure County is correct on the form -- If you get signatures from 5 counties, you need 5 forms.

Review what you got before you go to the state capitol to turn them in.

Many signatures are thrown out because of very small mistakes.
Let's Look at the areas of mistakes that might be made for the meeting
1. Make sure that every detail of everybody's signature is perfect
2. Do not use WB or ditto marks.
3. Make sure you use the Luzerne County form only for Luzerne County Signatories
4. If the signatory makes a mistake, draw a line through it and let them write it again.
5. It helps to check the data sheets vs. the signatures line for errors.

Why would a signature be contested? Here's why:

Signature Line Challenges -- the incumbent or other challenger wants to get all signatures thrown out claiming inaccuracies

1. Date on line not between Feb 16 & March 9
2. Signer is not a registered voter
3. Signer resides in wrong district (16 or 18)
4. Signature or data not completely legible -- ask them to do-over.
5. Multiple counties on same form – entire form gets thrown out.
6. Address is wrong / incomplete / missing address
7. Incomplete / missing dates / dates out of order
8. Ditto marks
9. Nickname or initials in place of full name
10. No cursive signature
11. Wrong / fraudulent signature*

Write notes on your notes such as these:

 *** We will have a meeting at my house on Feb. 27 or March 6, depending on how the signatures are coming in. I will bring a Notary public to notarize the signature petitions for the carriers. BK will pay for it. Do not get them notarized before then.

Don't forget to ask your relatives, close friends and those who you see all the time. We are looking for D, D17

Send Greemez an email so he can communicate with you
<greemez@comcast.net>

Chapter 5 Ballot Access: The Game is Rigged!

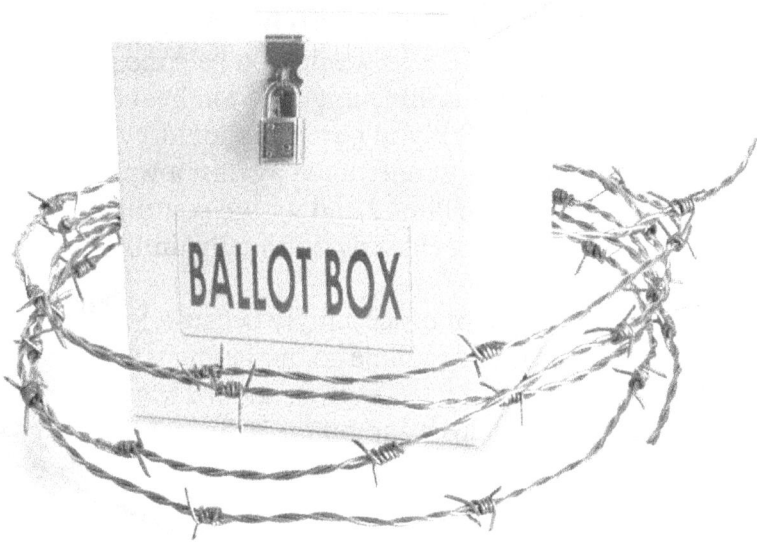

Try running for office!

BALLOT ACCESS: THE GAME IS RIGGED!

Please enjoy the excerpts of this essay by Mr. Brian Kelly.

Try running for Office in a state such as Pennsylvania, in which the political Incumbents and the establishment have the game rigged. Pennsylvania's corrupt state politicians have slanted the ballot-access table in favor of incumbents and against non-political regular citizens of the Commonwealth.

There are major trials and tribulations facing regular people who attempt to present themselves as candidates on any ballot for any office in the United States of America. The ballot access issue in Pennsylvania is one of the worst in the nation. It should not surprise anybody that the incumbent politicians make the laws that make it difficult for anybody to unseat them. There are many surprisingly restrictive ballot access laws in this country. The average citizen voter has no knowledge or concept of the extent of the problem until one day, he or she decides to put their hat in the ring and they run for office, hoping to give something back.

If you are so inclined, do you feel that you might actually be able to run unimpeded for an important office in Pennsylvania? Would you just go ahead and do it or would you be concerned that the weight of the political machine might be too heavily focused against your candidacy? If you gave it a shot, do you think you would be permitted to run unfettered against a well-established political class whose livelihood and whose continued excessive wealth depends on being elected continually until they die?

I thought I would run for office simply because I am an American and this is America. I have done so but let me tell you the road is unpaved. I formally ran for Congress and for Mayor. I was on the ballot for Congress in 2010 and on the ballot for Mayor of Wilkes-Barre in 2015. There is a lot of work in running for office and unless you become a politician, or the people stop bootlicking politicians by voting for them, a new candidate can expect nothing but misery and failure.

Do you wonder why so few people run for office? Surely you have neighbors who you think would be much better at leading our country, state, county, or city than the same old crew whose names make the ballot every election. I know first-hand why more good people choose to stay away from becoming elected officials. It is because the politicians control the playing field. If you think the game is rigged, you are right! The game is rigged.

There is a big reason why potential candidates for office do not simply emerge into the sunlight when they are so inclined to be the next Mayor, Governor, Senator, or Representative. It is the same reason that even Donald Trump and Bernie Sanders have learned in trying to become president. The game is rigged, at all levels.

The reason is that there are lots of impediments and major roadblocks that need to be carefully navigated. Those currently holding offices of and for the people, think they own the people.

Consider that there are no documented cases of an elected official, who in their first term or any term ever calls all citizens of the community together for a meeting to find some other good candidates to run.

It seems logical that we all would have been invited at some time to say, a church hall, so that a great leader could describe to us the process of becoming the next such and such from so and so. If we all wanted the best people to serve, would we not be encouraging our neighbors to come out and be welcomed to consider putting his or her hat in the ring to serve the people?

Too bad that we are deprived of having regular, ordinary citizens such as you and me, rather than *machine groomed politicians* be the candidates for the offices available in almost all elections. Over time, the political class through gerrymandering and restrictive ballot access laws, and special rules known only unto them, have made it difficult for anybody other than a crooked politician to get elected.

Politicians play the game and they eventually become experts. It is not by accident that the winners are almost always endorsed by the big Party machines, and let me tell you all, the machines are really big and are really powerful and tough to overcome. Regular Joe's and Josephine's are excluded in the process intentionally, but the methods are not entirely obvious. The fact that it costs a lot of money to compete is just one of the first obstacles.

For the money and the major effort, a newcomer has less than a slim chance to gain the nomination or win a general election. Once you put your hat in the ring, there is a lot of unexpected and unnecessary work and expense. It is not an accident that any candidate running for the first time feels that all of the politicians and the minions in government have their hands locked into his or her wallet.

It was not always that way and the founders did not intend it to be that way. Unfortunately, elected politicians have always had the power to make things easy for their next election regardless of its impact on democracy, the will of the people, and the good of the people. The founding fathers expected that the people would throw the bums out, but the bums have made it very difficult,

Their path to a reelection and a slot at the establishment perks table is much easier than your path to be newly elected. They use something that I would call a special "incumbent grease." The incumbent grease makes them quite slippery and it helps them to be impervious to the rot they create, through which those not as well connected must traverse.

It was not until the 1880's for example that paper ballots began to be printed by the government. Before then it was private entities who produced the ballots and even before then voice votes were used. In the 1880's official secret ballots came into being by government decree and that is when the ballot access issues for John Q Public began. It is funny how the government broke a system that had worked well for 100 years at that time. Government breaks a lot more than it fixes.

The elitists believed that only elitists should be able to run for public office and they set out to make sure that it was a task that most ordinary citizens would choose not to take up. Today as we see in Congress and the Senate, and even the Presidency, the sense of entitlement to the office held is so strong that the "elite" politicians believe that they know more than the people they serve.

They also know that it is so difficult for a newcomer to replace them that they no longer believe they have a requirement to do the people's will to be re-elected. Of course, that was before the recent populist movement that has Donald Trump and Ted Cruz and Bernie Sanders, ostensibly outsiders to the presidential process, doing so well today. To not be an incumbent in 2018 is now a major advantage for the people. But, will the establishment still have the power and the gall to direct the results? We'll see!

The TEA Party movement of 2009 from its first brew was unfairly defamed by the corrupt progressive media. Yet, it is the TEA Party, a term not mentioned much today in 2018, that built the foundation for today's populist movement that elected Donald Trump as President. This movement has brought us candidates who do not owe their allegiance to big donors or the Party machines.

Wikipedia, which is not respected by SWAMP dwellers and sometimes, but infrequently, gets it wrong, got this fact 100% right. It cites that historian Peter Argersinger pointed out that the 1880's reform "that conferred power on officials to regulate who may be on the ballot carried with it the danger that this power would be abused by officialdom and that legislatures controlled by the established political parties (specifically, the Republican and Democratic Parties), would enact restrictive ballot access laws to influence election outcomes, for partisan purposes, in order to ensure re-election of their own party's candidates." Peter Argersinger was 100% correct and my own story as a candidate confirms that.

As a candidate several times who paid a big price to be on the ballot, I can assure all Americans that the ballot access system provided by the states is not designed to let the most competent person through the maze. Thus, the people most often send the same scoundrels back to office rather than help new blood present its case. First of all, there are no ready forums to present one's case.

One would presume with no knowledge that the United States would have the fairest ballot access rules in the world of countries that practice a form of democracy. But, this is not true. The United States has been criticized by the Organization for Security and Cooperation in Europe (OSCE) for its harsh ballot access laws in the past. From my own experience, the US has not really lightened up on the rules that prevent ordinary citizens to get on the ballot. The corrupt press never reports on it as the press is part of the problem, not the solution.

I wrote a book on Amazon titled The Day the Free Press Died that shows how bad the free press has become: https://www.amazon.com/Day-Free-Press-Died-integrity-ebook/dp/B079F37H7G/ref=sr_1_1?s=books&ie=UTF8&qid=1532215065&sr=1-1&keywords=free+press+died

The OSCE thinks PA has bad laws. This is one place in which it appears the Brits have us beat. In their political science model of a healthy two-party system, every candidate for Parliament faces the same ballot-access hurdle-- a simple filing fee. Not only is it free but candidates from all parties are granted two free mailings to all the voters. That's not the end of the fairness. Every candidate also gets some free TV and radio time. It's almost as if the Brits want real people not just politicians to be able to achieve an office in Parliament.

We have the same access here if you have the big bucks and lots of spare time. In Britain, they have legal equality between all the parties and it seems to work. Our system seems to be corrupt. As Donald Trump says quite well and quite often: "The system is rigged." Trump is right!

You saw what happened in Colorado, Trump said. It's a fix. We thought we were having an election and a number of months ago, they decide to do it by you know what, right? They said well do it by delegate. Aw, isn't that nice? And the delegates were all there waiting. And, one of them tweeted out today and said today, by mistake, and then they withdrew it, something to the effect of See, never Trump.

Mr. Trump spoke at a rally with over 10,000 supporters who packed the Times Union Center, a sports and concert venue in downtown Albany: I'm hundreds of delegates ahead but the system, folks, is rigged. It's a rigged, disgusting, dirty system.

As a person who has run four times in this dirty system, I more than agree. It is rigged to benefit long term dirty corrupt politicians who in this election, are known simply as "The Establishment."

Even at the local level, when I ran for Mayor in 2015 and was on the ballot, I requested in early 2015 that Mayor Leighton open City Hall for a meet the candidates night twice a month for the few months of the election season. Each mayoral candidate would speak for an hour and each Council candidate would also get time to speak.

The Mayor said the City could not sponsor such events as it was against the law. I have two sons who are lawyers, and this simply is not true. Regardless, the Mayor acted like he owned City Hall, not like he was merely renting it with the people's permission until the end of his term. I beg to differ that a Mayor or public official cannot choose to help the electoral process.

But, we all know it is very difficult fighting City Hall. The newspapers are AWOL. Radio stations permit call-ins for brief periods but the local TV stations including Public TV offer nothing for aspiring candidates. The message is to get your wallet out and pay to permit the people to learn to know you. The Fourth estate is dead in Wilkes-Barre PA and for the most part across the country.

In 2010, when I ran for Congress, the incumbent, who seemingly was responsible for funding allocations for Public TV, decided that there would be no public forum or debates on Public TV for the Congressional House Race! Is it not convenient to be the well-known incumbent and have the power to limit your opponent's opportunities to take your job?

The noted scholar John Henry Wigmore, professor of law at Northwestern Univ. from 1901 to 1929, who ultimately was dean of the law faculty had some big-time opinions on fair elections. In his earlier life (1880s) Wigmore had been a leader for election law reform, especially the secret voting method and ballot access laws. His suggestion in my opinion makes sense. He recommended that as few as ten signatures would be an appropriate requirement for nomination to gain access to the official ballot for a legislative office.

For Congress in PA, a candidate needs 1000 signatures plus 1000 more signatures to cover signature challenges. For the US Senate it is 2000 signatures. For Mayor, one needs 100 signatures plus 100 more to cover challenges. I dare you to try to get a signature from anybody for anything. See how easy it is. Candidates get three weeks to get all signatures while still going to work every day. Each signature petition sheet of 50 maximum and 1 minimum must be notarized. That is another $5.00 to $10.00 per signature.

So, does that make Pennsylvania law 100 times better than the suggestion of this sage legal scholar who thinks ten signatures are sufficient? Let me repeat myself on the requirement. As noted, in PA, one hoping to become a candidate on the ballot for Congress on the Republican or Democrat side must attain 1000 signatures plus 1000 more for challenges in less than three weeks. I submit that this is regardless of how many snow storms there may have been.

All of this hard work, 100 times more than Wigmore's suggestion is necessary to be a candidate for US Representative for either party. Incumbents illegally use their staff to get the signatures or the Party pays as much as $5.00 to $10.00 per signature to have professionals canvas for them. Regular citizens have no such staffs.

At about six to ten signatures per hour, one certainly cannot expect to hold a job and live a normal life if trying to get the signatures by oneself. The clear objective of such as system is to limit the access to the ballot so that normal people say, "no way," and politician after politician has his or her way with the people's treasury.

When the signatures are submitted, it is also clear that the objective is to eliminate signatures, not to verify the real citizens who signed the petitions. They may be valid citizens, thereby making their attestation valid but if they make a mistake in their own name or the city or the date or their apartment #, their attestation of a candidate is thrown in the garbage. In a recent US Senate primary in Pennsylvania, Joseph Vodvarka's signatures were challenged by the opportunistic Joe Sestak.

When I first wrote this essay, Mr. Sestak hoped to deny Pennsylvanians a candidate who is of the people and not of the political class. He hoped to chop hundreds of signatures from Vodvarka's submitted petitions. He wanted them marked invalid so that Mr. Vodvarka would lose his right to be on the ballot.

That's how bad it is. Since then, I learned that on April 1, the Courts favored Sestak. What a sham. The system is rigged.

Sestak almost immediately took Vodvarka to court, so it would cost Vodvarka money to defend his petitions with over 2000 signatures. Sestak, a well-tuned in politician says more than 60 percent of the Vodvarka voter signatures are invalid. Sestak was not known at the time for being a handwriting expert. Yet, he claimed the signatures were flawed and should not be counted. I say if they can find ten good signatures, Vodvarka should be in! What human being can get 4000 signatures in three weeks? Think about it.

Most courts are smarter than the politics often employed by jurists in making decisions. The PA Court ruled against Vodvarka.

U.S. Senate candidates have a tougher time to get signatures than House candidates. Instead of 1000, they need to collect 2,000 signatures to qualify to be on the ballot. Those petition signers must be registered to vote in the county where they reside and be of the same political party as the candidate. Joe Vodvarka had submitted 2,744 signatures, which ought to be enough, except in a rigged system, to have him on the ballot.

Prior to the Commonwealth Court hearing arguments on Sestak's challenge, attorneys for Vodvarka and Sestak reached an agreement and stipulated to the court that 558 signatures on Vodvarka's petitions were invalid. As long as he was on the ballot, why would Vodvarka care that he only had 200 or so to spare. That left Vodvarka with 2,186 signatures. But the Commonwealth Court chopped off another 400 signatures so Vodvarka could not run on the ballot with 1800 signatures. What kind of guy does that make Sestak? What kind of lousy system would authorize such a perpetration of justice?

Political pundits have often said that the poll tax is the worst tax possible as it denies people the right to vote. It is my humble opinion that the method of using exorbitant numbers of signatures and arbitrary signature cancellations is worse than a poll tax as it denies the citizens the very candidates that would make an election with just politicians running, into a real election. A politician's objective, such as Joe Sestak, is to eliminate candidates not to verify that they are capable of serving.

Speaking of taxes, to help get 1000 signatures, one can ask for the county database or state database. I called the state and was routed back and forth and then each time; the phone was conveniently disconnected. For my part, I got the pleasure of dialing again but since time is important, I chose not to work with the state. The state database cost $20.00 or so I had been told.

District 11 [Before the recent changes to District 17] in Pennsylvania consisted of all or part of five different counties -- Carbon, Columbia, Monroe, Lackawanna, and Luzerne. To get the databases for these counties, they must be obtained from the counties one by one, for a sum of $50.00 per CD or $250.00. To capture one signature on a petition in each of the five counties--a total of just 5 signatures--would cost approximately $10,00 in Notary Public fees per sheet or $50.00 to have all five signatures notarized.

Why is this a requirement when the State does not accept the notarized affidavit---the word of the Notary, anyway? Vodvarka's were all notarized but the court did not accept the Notary's attestations. The answer is because it is effective harassment for anybody who dares challenge the powers that be. But, you already know that.

Each House petition holds 50 signatures, so it would take 20 perfect petitions to reach 1000 signatures at a cost of $200.00. Since, at least 1500 signatures are recommended as many will be eliminated rather than verified, this cost is at best $300.00. With signature circulators working on behalf of every candidate, many of the sheets have no more than ten signatures. If all had just ten signatures, this would be 100 sheets and the cost would be $1000.00 for the notarization of the signatures.

What purpose does this serve?

Additionally, there is a filing fee of $150.00 to be able to submit the petitions and be duly registered as a candidate to be placed on the ballot. They don't take Visa or Master Card. They do not take personal checks. So, I had to go to the bank to get a $150.00 cashier's check made out perfectly to the State of PA or they would not accept it. More harassment.

Then, though there were five Voters services offices in District 11, ostensibly because this is a National election, the full petition, a notarized affidavit (another $10.00) and the cashier's check had to be taken to Harrisburg (two hours each way plus mileage cost -- say another $50.00) to a specific room to be processed.

In the directions from Harrisburg, to add insult to injury, I found it comforting that there was a caution after noting that the signature period was from February 16 to March 9. The caution said, "Do not wait until the last minute." In other words, the office is closing at 5:00 P.M. on March 9 so you better be in, processed, and out by 5:00 P.M. When I arrived on a Tuesday, I thought I was OK. Only about forty signatures were discounted. Despite all the obstacles I made it onto the ballot for Congress. .

Many citizens do not know how difficult it is for a non-politico to run for any office in Pennsylvania or they would insist that the rules be more reasonable. We have our corrupt state lawmakers to blame for that and they must fix this even before, in our contempt for them, we replace them all. I will do my best, I can assure you to enable ballot access for all so that we the people are not cursed to have only politicians to choose from in our elections.

Speaking of citizens and the requirement for 1000 signatures. It is my understanding that the incumbent merely instructs his staff to get signatures and it is not that big of a deal. If the staff is only minimally involved the incumbent can attend a number of political events during the three-week period with hundreds of willing signatures available at each event. The lone wolf, the average Joe, our own John Q. Public, does not have it quite so easy.

In my case, I called a number of establishments to see if I could bring my petition inside and quietly ask people to sign to help grant me ballot access. I learned something in this process. Some establishments are quite gracious and assist in this civic duty of enabling ballot access for citizens of NEPA, who are not part of the machine.

Of course, they would also permit those of the machine and that is fair. Some establishments are not so gracious and they either put me off or took it up the flagpole only to have the owner decree that they did not engage in such politics. For me in these cases, I concluded that they had an alignment with the machine, which I did not have. Knocking on doors is the toughest way to get signatures.

I am running for the US Senate in 2018

Until I die, I may continue to run for some political office. What I will not do is spend money or raise money any more. I will have a web site, write articles, send editorials to newspapers, and I will speak when invited.

When elected to the US Senate this year, I will serve one term and If I am in good health in six years, I may go for one more. That ought to be more than enough.

I spent close to $5000 of my own money to run for Congress in 2010. When I ran for Mayor in 2015, I thought it would be easier. I spent about $6000 but family and friends donated about $3000 so altogether, I am out at least $8,000 and probably more because of PA ballot access laws. I won't do this again this way for sure. I wish I had the cash back for a few more family vacations. Yet, here I am running for office again. How am I going to pull that off? Quick-answer -- Write me in!

If voters tuned into write-in ballot laws, and there was a listing service so that anybody could announce that they were running as a write-in candidate, we can again have a democratic republic as the founders intended. It costs nothing to run as a write-in. All you have to do is make sure that the potential voters know about you.

So, with the listing service, instead of having to get 1500 signatures, anybody can run for Congress. Because it would be so easy and be no charge, citizens would have a huge selection of candidates. We should talk more about this... don't you think?

In the meantime, I bought a web site to handle write-in ballots. Well, it really does not handle write-in ballots as you still have to vote at your polling place. However, it is a place in which any write-in candidate can list his or her name so that any citizen can access the site to find out who they are. That way, ladies and gentlemen, we are not stuck with politicians as public officials.

The name of this web site is www.writeinballots.com. I have yet to fire it up but some day!

God bless America!

Vote for the Underdog... Just write in **Brian Kelly** this time. It's that easy! Next time send out a memo like this, and we'll all be voting for you and it will not cost you a dime.

With 165-books, Brian W. Kelly is the most-published and thus the leading conservative author in America. He is an outspoken and eloquent expert on solutions to help America and Americans Though a Democrat, he is a JFK Democrat. One of his pet peeves is the chicanery and deceit of RINOS and DINOS on all Americans.

About Brian Kelly:

Brian Kelly is a former IBM Senior Systems Engineer and Retired Professor of Business and Information Technology (BIT) at Marywood University in Scranton, PA. He was a candidate for US Congress from PA District 11 in 2010. Kelly was also a candidate running for Mayor in his home town of Wilkes-Barre PA in 2015. Brian still manages his own IT business (www.kellyconsulting.com), and he has recently completed his 166th book, available at amazon.com/author/brianwkelly.

Brian is currently running for office as a write-in candidate as a Democrat for the US Senate to Pennsylvania. You can check out his campaign web site at www.kellyforussenate.com). The good news according to Kelly is that when running as a write-in, there are virtually no campaign expenses.

Thank you for being part of the quiet populist revolution to save America.

Chapter 6 Elect Brian Kelly as Your Senator from PA.

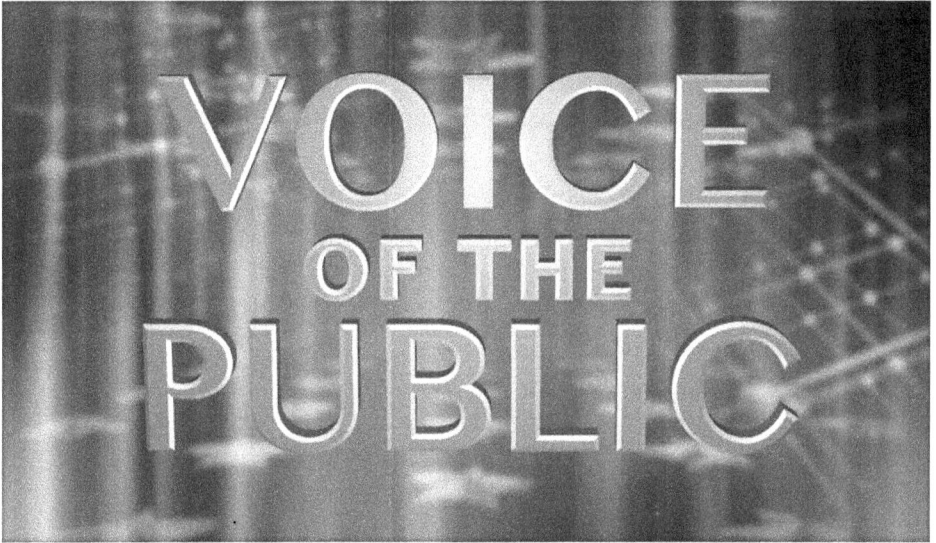

About you

Make sure you highlight your finest points. If you were Brian Kelly, this might be some of what you would say.

Brian Kelly is married to the former Patricia Piotroski, and the couple resides in Northeastern Pennsylvania as they have all their married life of forty-one years. They are the proud parents of three wonderful adult children, Brian, Michael, and Katie. Ben, the family canine, and Buddy, the family feline, reside with Pat and Brian, but are loved by all.

Brian Kelly was born and "raised" in Wilkes-Barre PA. He attended St. Boniface Grade School and Meyers High School. Brian was both a pitcher and a catcher on the Meyers High Baseball team and he was active in many school clubs as well as the student council.

Brian competed for an academic scholarship to King's College and was awarded a four-year academic scholarship grant, a National Defense Student Loan, and a work-study job. The job in the federal work-study program helped him make up a $50.00 per year tuition shortfall. Tuition was $475.00 per semester. Scholarship was $250, and loan was $200. Brian is most grateful to King's College for the Academic scholarship and to the Federal Government for the loan and work-study assistance. His degree was the difference between a successful business life and a blue-collar job.

Brian graduated cum laude ranked #29 of 382 from King's with a degree in Data Processing, the pre-cursor degree to Business Information Technology. While at King's, Kelly was a member of two honor societies, the King's Aquinas Society, and the Delta Epsilon Sigma National Honor Society. Brian played varsity Baseball for the Monarchs as a catcher / pinch hitter, and then as a starting pitcher in his Junior and Senior years.

After King's, he joined the IBM Corporation as a Computer Science Systems Assistant where he spent 23 years before retiring, under a special program, as a Senior Systems Engineer. During his IBM career, Kelly received his M.B.A. summa cum laude in Accounting and Finance from Wilkes University. After his time at IBM, Brian accepted a position with College Misericordia as its Chief Technology Director / Internal IT Consultant. At the same time, he initiated his own IT Consulting Practice, Kelly Consulting.

After building the College Misericordia campus network, its connection to the Internet, its email and its Web servers, Kelly left College Misericordia and moved on to spend full time in his own IT business consulting practice. In 2004, Kelly joined the faculty of Marywood University and, in addition to maintaining his consulting practice, Brian served Marywood as an Assistant Professor of Business Information Technology and as its IBM i system technology assistant to the Business Information Technology Faculty.

Contact campaign@yourwebsite.com

An Entreaty to vote for Brian Kelly

Fellow Citizens of Northeastern Pennsylvania, I would like to present myself as a Candidate to be your US Senator for the State of Pennsylvania. As you know, this seat is currently held by Bob Casey

Jr. but not for long. I am running as a write-in candidate, a Democrat against Mr. Casey in the General Election on November 6, 2018.

I am proud to say that--but for a few years as an independent living in Utica, NY, I would be a lifetime Democrat and a lifetime resident of Northeastern PA. Right after I earned my Bachelor of Science from King's College at the age of 21, I competed in a tough job marketplace, and I had the good fortune of being hired to work as a Systems Engineer at IBM in Utica, New York. For two years, I lived in Utica as a registered Independent.

My dad, a lifetime Democrat, was very conservative and good man. He was a staunch believer in the importance of labor unions to help the working man in America. He worked as heating specialist at R. A. Davis in Wilkes-Barre and then as laborer at Stegmaier Brewery on "Brewery Hill" in Wilkes-Barre for thirty-one years until the Stegmaier label was purchased by the Lion Incorporated. At that time, the Lion proudly brewed Gibbons Beer.

[G-I-B-B-O-N-S, pure refreshing Gibbons. If it's Gibbons, it's good—so the next time you should say gimme gimme gimme Gibbons!]

That is the essence of the 1960's Gibbons commercial.

Stegmaier of course brewed a number of different beers, including Stegmaier Beer, Ale, Porter, and Bach. When I was in my twenties, the "Brewery" brought back Liebotschaner, a finely crafted and aged old-time Stegmaier formulation. The company made its beer from fresh grains and hops and malt and it aged all of its products in huge vats on the left side of Market St. as one headed up Brewery Hill.

[So! If you want a beer that's mellow, a beer that is really grand, say hey, make mine Stegmaier, the gold medal beer of the land. And, so at home, or club, or tap room; always order the beer that they cheer. Served just right; mellow, cool, and light, Stegmaier Gold Medal Beer.]

The paragraph above is the essence of the 1960's Stegmaier commercial.

My dad was pretty good at what he did and he took his work seriously. For a number of years before its demise, Stegmaier had one of the fastest canning machines in Pennsylvania. My dad operated this behemoth single-handedly. For its day, it was an awesome machine. It put out 600 cans per minute. That's even fast according to today's standards. My dad was quite a guy.

My father and I regularly had discussions about beliefs and ideologies and which candidate truly was best for official jobs, at the local, state, and federal levels. More often than not, he and I were on the same page. My dad's philosophy was that you should always vote for the best candidate for the job, not simply the political party. These discussions eventually prompted me to cancel my registration as an independent and become a Democrat. In Pennsylvania, Independents have no voice in the primary elections.

Lots of discontent is not only brewing; it's boiling-over.

There is a storm of discontent content brewing across the United States. You can feel it wherever you go. Regular Americans are beginning to pay attention to what our Congressional representatives have been doing against our will in Washington, D.C. Politics and government, and their collective effect on what's happening in America have become regular dinner table topics.

I know few people today who think President Obama was a good president. In fact, most of my friends have him slotted as one of the worst presidents ever. I think they are right! Sometimes particular Democrats do not have it right. It is OK to be upset. It is OK to show some disgust for what these knaves such as Bob Casey Jr. have done to America. It's OK to be disgusted, Me too! That's why I am running for the US Senate.

I am still a Democrat because like you I am hoping it becomes a party that mirrors the people rather than going so far left we are all left behind. The leaders of the Democratic Party have betrayed the common man, such as you and me; but none of us writing or reading this paragraph are dead and so we can change the Democratic Party, so it no longer is a party of identity politics that separates Americans under the guise of diversity. Instead for the sake of American unity, we can all join together under the huge umbrella of the US Constitution and reject those leaders who have led us down a path to perdition.

What's not OK is to sit around and let these same elitist establishment types come back again in 2019 to inflict more harm on the American people. Vote them out. You have the power! We have the power!

I decided to run for the US Senate as a write-in candidate because somebody has to represent US. I am a write-in because it means that I do not have to bootlick the rich and powerful for donations. We need change more now than when we thought we needed change and brought in Obama. God gave us Donald Trump as a model for how things should be done.

What we do not need is the kind of change that exalts one man and attempts to silence a nation. I ask you to vote "for the people" on November 6 of this year. Vote out the proponents of big, intrusive, freedom-taking government and all the politicians will disappear overnight.

It seems the kind of change we have been getting from our former anti-American President and the corrupt Congress was good only for the government and the high-paid bureaucrats. It is not the right formula for freedom-loving Americans. While you and I are asking to have government less involved in our daily lives, Congress and our former president were throwing one freedom-stealing regulation after another on us on their way to making this a socialist nation. This Congress does not represent the people.

We can fix that. All we have to do is vote them out. The people think that they are powerless, yet we have all the power. I am running for the US Senate and I am a Democrat. Please do not vote for anybody who has hurt Donald Trump's presidency in the general election.

Don't count on other states to get this job done without our participation. It all starts at home. For US, that is Pennsylvania. Our time has come. Good-by to all the incumbents who are contributing to the downfall of America. Good-by to Bob Casey, an embarrassment to Northeastern PA. Hold your collective noses and then vote him out!

I would hope that by learning about who I am and where I am from and what I stand for, you will conclude that we have unity of purpose. I am one of the regular people in life. I believe that it is my time to serve and if you will permit me, I would be honored to be your Senator for all the regular people in Pennsylvania.

Things worth repeating are worth repeating

Here is some stuff from a press release by the campaign that is very readable and as are most of Brian Kelly's writings. It calls the people to action. Brian believes that we the people have no choice than to be more than mere passers-by in a country being dragged into submission by people who hate America.

*** PRESS RELEASE ***
BRIAN KELLY ANNOUNCES HIS CANDIDACY FOR the US SENATE FROM PENNSYLVAMIA.

Kelly Says It Is Time to Return the Government to The People!

Brian Kelly, a former IBM Senior Systems Engineer and Assistant Professor of Business and Information Technology (BIT) at Marywood University in Scranton, announced his write-in candidacy for the US Senate .

Kelly has promised that he will run as an independent write-in candidate as a Democrat in the general election since he did not compete in the primary election. Brian asks all Democrats to vote for him in the general election as he will serve all voters well.

Brian Kelly has worked in the private sector all his life. He hates what is happening to the US and to Pennsylvania and his solutions are designed to make it better.

Brian Kelly expresses his reason for running for public office in these simple terms: "to return our government back to the people." Kelly notes that government spending is out of control and that only a change in leadership can turn government away from more unpopular tax-payer funded bailouts, crippling taxes and government-takeovers. Casey, a successful lawyer of course is for more spending and for more taxing of those who earn a living in Pennsylvania.

Brian sees the solution as "We must create jobs, not destroy them. The policies of Bob Casey and Barack Obama were killing US businesses before Donald Trump was elected. Like many, I fear the building of a huge, never ending bureaucracy wherever you look." Brian believes that Bob Casey must go so a Trump-Friendly legislature can be in place to help America.

Kelly finds government as the only "industry" which prospered before Trump. Now, all of America is moving forward, and those who are in the way of the Make America Great Again agenda, both Republicans and Democrats need to be replaced. That's why you need to write-in B-R-I-A-N K-E-L-L Y.

Brian fears the seemingly predestined government takeover of healthcare, the disrupting of the doctor patient relationships, and the bankrupt notion of repressive energy tax legislation and the destruction of the industry that produces America's most abundant energy source-coal. He is concerned that all of this excessive government, which the incumbent supports, will make it tough for Americans to live like Americans. "You can be assured that I will work to stop these flawed changes brought about by poor leadership." Kelly said.

Kelly said that in order to restore the economy, "a brand-new Congress must be committed to getting government to stop micro-managing the economy." They must support Donald Trump to help America.

Government takeovers, national debt, a huge deficit, and the major job killing regulations of the Obama / Casey administration are being rejected summarily by all Americans.

Pennsylvanians will be hurt even more than others by the shutdown of coal and an "energy tax" since many PA communities still have a viable coal industry. Casey is not for Pennsylvanians and his votes could kill the energy industry in PA through taxes or restrictive regulations.

Besides being unfriendly to Pennsylvania business and industry, the only creators of lasting jobs, Bob Casey is vulnerable in 2018 because his positions mirror those of the unpopular Chuck Schumer, Nancy Pelosi, and Maxine Watters. Why would our Senator, against constituent write-ins, support Obamacare and other socialist, budget busting legislation?

Kelly boasts that he has the backing of no political machine and he is taking no political contributions. "It sure should save a lot of time, not having to run fund-raisers." Kelly said. He is proud to say that his total war chest from contributions is $0.00, and he is nowhere close to having to pay the "Obama / Casey Rich Tax."

Kelly feels his message will be brought forth now that he has made it known that he is a serious contender for the nomination and for election in November 2018. By writing in the name Brian Kelly, the people will recognize that a regular old "John Doe," not a political operative has made himself available to the people.

Kelly once had a lot of affinity for the "Tea Party People," and those like you and I, who are not part of a named group but who nonetheless have been justifiably enraged at the unresponsiveness of our government. From Kelly's perspectives, the left made the tea party seem like a bunch of life perverts and nobody complained loud enough to know they that it was not the tea, it was the name and it was the people, regular people who the left hoped to discredit but could not because they were simply you and me. .

Kelly said: "At this stage of my life, I see things that can be so much better if Americans had better representation. I feel in many ways like George Bailey from the Building and Loan in "It's a Wonderful Life," seeing the face of the corrupt Mr. Potter in too many hallways of government.

I'd like to take the spirit of WW II Brigadier General Jimmy Stewart (real life) as George Bailey and keep all the Potters out of government for an awful long time--even if it means that I have to put in a few years myself."

Kelly is not interested in a career in politics and when elected will stay for just one or at most two terms. Kelly says: "A regular person holding an office becomes a politician when trying to be reelected."

When the constituents of Pennsylvania get in the "voting booth," no matter how many dollars Bob Casey has spent to advance his candidacy, the only thing voters must remember is two words forming one name, Brian Kelly. It is just ten letters and a space. When they write that name in BRIAN KELLY on the ballot, things will begin to change almost immediately.

"The voters will ask themselves, 'is he a politician?' and the answer of course is 'no.' As voters across the US are trying to free themselves from machine politics, with votes to the highest bidders, Brian Kelly is betting that in Northeastern PA, being 'of the people' will matter more than anything on November 6, 2019. " Kelly said.

As an author, Brian Kelly wishes he were not so old that he has been able to write 165 books, many of which are in the high-tech field. He is tickled, however, that he has written over sixty books since 2010 hoping to convince his fellow Democrats that we must not permit the power brokers in the Democratic Party to ever win again. We can still be good Democrats if we force the power brokers to be more human.

In 2007, Brian Kelly began research for his first book about government. In 2008, he released these first efforts with a book titled, Taxation Without Representation, sold on the Internet at such places as Amazon.com and Barnes & Noble. He has updated the Taxation book and wrote many new patriotic books since then.

These are the product of major research as well as his clear opinions as to how the country has gotten off course. Two of his newest books include Wilkes-Barre PA Return to Glory! and The Constitution 4 Dummmies, and Millennials are people too !!! . Those who think the thoughts of the people do not matter, will not read any of these books

Kelly is an ardent defender of the Constitution and in many of his books, he adds appendices with the full text of the US Constitution and other founding documents.

By visiting this website at www.kellyforussenate.com or by reading his books, available at amazon.com/author/brianwkelly, it is easy to know that Brian Kelly stands where you stand on the issues of the day. He sounds like one of US because he is one of US.

Brian Kelly asks all Democrats and Republicans in Pennsylvania to write-in Brian Kelly in the General Election on November 6. Two words, both are needed for a valid write-in. "I promise that you will have change --- this time it will be change that you can live with." And, won't that be a grand day. ---------

Best wishes for a better America from Brian Kelly.

Sometimes it helps to see things again in summary form:

Brian Kelly's Summary Background:

- E. L. Meyers High, W-B, PA, with honors
- B. S. from King's College cum laude
- M. B. A. from Wilkes University magna cum laude
- 23 years with IBM Corporation as Senior Systems Engineer
- 15 Year Ongoing Consultancy--Business and IT Consultant
- 5 years Misericordia University, Chief Tech Officer
- 7 years with Marywood University -- Assistant Professor, Business Information technology
- Author—164 books, Hundreds of magazine articles

Brian Kelly believes in the effort to restore reverence for God and respect for the unalienable rights to life and liberty in America.

Brian Kelly believes and understands the notion of self-government of, by, and for the people – as well as our moral, physical, and economic sovereignty. Kelly has written four books in this regard:

Taxation Without Representation; *Obama's Seven Deadly Sins* - ; and Healthcare Accountability. Included in each of the first three books is a full copy of the Constitution of the United States, something that we all should keep in our hands in these trying times. Kelly penned another book titled: Jobs! Jobs! Jobs! in 2010.

Altogether he has written 164 books. Most were penned between 2010 to 2018. All are available from amazon.com/author/brianwkelly

Brian Kelly is easy to understand. He is in synch with the Donald Trump agenda. He is an advocate of a complete overhaul of our taxing system and the abolishment of the 16th Amendment, thereby eliminating the tax code and the IRS. The Fair Tax has many advantages over the current income tax system. The Fair tax seems to have the most advantages of all other options, but even the Flat tax is far better than our current income tax system

- Brian Kelly is an advocate of strong border security
- Brian Kelly is ready to declare our nation's reliance on God as fundamental.
- Brian Kelly will work to protect our unalienable rights to life, liberty, and private property.
- Brian Kelly will help restore and protect our constitutional republican form of government.
- Brian Kelly will work to protect the institution of marriage and the traditional family.
- Brian Kelly will work to protect our national sovereignty, military strength, and border security.

The rest of this book describes Brian Kelly's candidacy so that as had been announced in the past by those against Mr. Kelly, nobody can say that Brian Kelly is not the best candidate for America.

Chapter 7 Why is Brian Kelly Running for the US Senate

For your campaign, you may want to repeat things to be sure that the public has your message.

Question: Why are you running for the US Senate?
Answer: That is a very good question?

As a husband and father, my family was very important in this decision to run for office again. In 2008, I considered running and my family and I discussed it at length and I decided not to run. In 2010, I put a team together, and I saved some money and my family gave me encouragement, though they still had some trepidation about the potential impact on our family unit. We'd like to remain reasonably private and regular people. At the same time, there were other factors.

This year, eight years after I held the #1 position on the ballot for the Democratic Primary, I am running for the US Senate as a write-in candidate, because of a number of reasons. I am running as a write-in because I simply cannot afford to try to outspend the fat campaign war-chest amassed for Bob Casey. So, I am running a campaign on the cheap but with your help, I will prove that money does not trump the will of the people.

My family agrees that things are even worse for Americans this time around and Bob Casey's support for Chuck Schumer is making them worse. I would be happy to defer my candidacy to a like-minded person if one shows up. Short of that there are a lot of things that are wrong, with our country, and I would love the opportunity to get my hands dirty to help fix them. I am at the right time of my life and I see no reason why I should stand by and watch as my family's liberties, both economic and civil, are being wiped out by our own government.

Reagan had a sense of humor

You may remember Ronald Reagan's great sense of humor. Reagan, for example is credited with a number of sayings. Without me offering any commentary, you can learn a lot about why I am running for the US Senate from the fact that I really do love the following Reagan quotes.

"The nine most terrifying words in the English language are: 'I'm from the government and I'm here to help.'"

"Approximately 80 percent of our air pollution stems from hydrocarbons released by vegetation, so let's not go overboard in setting and enforcing tough emission standards from man-made sources."

"I've noticed that everyone who is for abortion has already been born."

"I am not worried about the deficit. It is big enough to take care of itself."

[Brian Kelly adds that Ronald Reagan never met Barack Obama]

"Politics is supposed to be the second-oldest profession. I have come to realize that it bears a very close resemblance to the first."

Does that help you know where I stand on those issues? There is a whole menu on this site. It is called "Platform Points." It discusses just about any point in my platform and offers where I stand on it.

In life, we are often told that we must be for something, not just against things. I am for a lot of things but one of my best ways of describing why I am running for Congress is to speak in the negative. "I do not want the government controlling my life." Yes, there is a corollary to that precept: "I do not want the government controlling your life."

I can recall some great people in my life making comments that now make so much sense. For example, Dennis Grimes Senior from Fulton Street in Wilkes-Barre, who, when told that Congress did not get much done this term, would always say: "good!" Then, of course with the twinkle in his Irish eyes, he would add a little priceless gem to make the sentence end well, and I would smile. How profound he was.

Each time Congress meets we lose more freedom. There are too many people who think that you should do this, and you should do that. It is bad news when they get into office. They want to make sure you do it and they have the power to make laws to make it mandatory. I want to let you alone to lead your own life, and I hope if you are in similar circumstance, that you will let me alone to lead my life.

I believe that freedom is our most important gift. Our forefathers shed their blood for our freedom and liberty. Freedom has no real limits but being a good person does add restrictions to freedom.

For example, I believe that in many and possibly most cases, a particular individual's freedom ends where another person's freedom begins. So, there will always be disputes between people and so it is OK to have some rules that help arbitrate man's behavior to his fellow man. My favorite rule book was created by the Founders. It is called the Constitution. Barack Obama and the 111th through 114th Congresses think they know better than the rules in this book and that is one major source of the angst in this country.

The fewer impositions of government on the people, the better. Government should get out of lives. We can handle salt, and sugar, and heat and cold. Government should worry about roads, bridges, traffic, and defense and a few other limited items.

I see no reason, for example to have a government law that outlaws beer, or two-ply toilet tissue, or red hair, or tattoos. I see no reason for laws that command that I must do something such as attend church services on Sundays -- or not attend or turn off my air conditioner in the summer (car or home) because somebody else wants me to save energy. I would not want to be commanded to use Dr. X as my family physician instead of Dr. Y. I surely would not want to have a visit scheduled with Dr. Kevorkian.

I would not want to have to use gasohol when gasoline or an alternative energy source suits my tastes. I would not want to have to buy health insurance, a pair of mittens, blue socks, a notepad, or cough medicine if I am not so inclined. I want liberty. I want freedom to make my own choices in life. On everything but abortion, I am pro-choice. On this issue I am pro Mom and pro Baby!

For me, it really is all about freedom, which is the positive of "no government control." I do not want government monitoring or controlling of my life from womb to tomb or any other area in between. I have written twenty-some additional books between my first run for Congress and now, many of which include a full copy of the Constitution of the United States.

The Constitution was created in order to form a "more perfect union," since it corrected a number of flaws in the Articles of Confederation. It is not perfect, but it is lots better than Nancy Pelosi and Harry Reid and Barack Obama making up freedom-destroying rules on the fly, as they go along.

My campaign is a very new campaign and for many it will not seem like much of a campaign. That's OK, the founding fathers would love it. If the truth be known, there is no real "campaign," just a bunch of friends who help me with great advice and my very active keyboard where I pen letters to the editor, press releases and essays for my web site. Thank you for reading this one. I hope to be able to select some "free" events in which to participate, but they are not offered frequently as incumbent politicians know that the more you know about me, the less you will like them.

The vast percentage of the people I know believe that we must fight back against a monstrous, out of control government. Those who know me believe that I would make a difference in Washington, and though they have cautioned that nobody gets elected without putting together at least a little machine, they enjoy the fact that we are doing this without any machine and with no contributions.

In 2010 my little team and I went out over three weeks and brought in 1516 signatures though I needed only 1000. Only! Try and get them. I will never do that again as I had to shut down my life and the lives of too many friends. We were out getting signatures but since all of us have some type of gainful employment, we could not have an exhaustive campaign and did not and will not try to knock on doors. It is tough enough just penning these articles.

Thank you for "listening." Don't forget to vote on November 6, 2018

Chapter 8 It's Tough Being Unknown!

"THE BIGGEST MISTAKE YOU COULD EVER MAKE IS BEING TOO AFRAID TO MAKE ONE."

~UNKNOWN

-EmilysQuotes.Com-

Everybody knows somebody sometime

It is not such a good thing when "everybody knows somebody sometime" and you are not on the list. When you are the new guy, sometimes the press forgets.

Many of your friends will ask you how you hope to get known if you live in one of the sixty-seven counties that make up Pennsylvania. Let me tell you, it is tough without major political financing. But, you must persevere with press releases, letters to the media, and make a speech whenever asked. To get the attention of the Press, a candidate must first "press" his nose against the glass of the media outlets (Newspaper, Radio, and TV) to get their attention. I am doing that with this book and a number of press releases and letters.

Unfortunately for unknown and not-well financed candidates, in my experience in having run unsuccessfully three times, the priority of the management of media outlets is to maintain their viability by bringing in ad revenue and not giving up space or time to citizen candidates. Know that it will not be smooth sailing, but nothing ventured, nothing gained.

Fortunately, I can set up and manage web sites and I can use Facebook. Therefore, I can reach web surfers without any cost. This time, I will not have a Donate Button to accept contributions but that is OK as I won't need an accountant when it is over to figure out the financial statements. Because it is a state-wide election yard signs in the local community will not be effective, so I will save on that.

In their article, Journalism in the Digital Age, five Stanford (cs.stanford.edu) authors-- Danny Crichton, Ben Christel, Aaditya Shidham, Alex Valderrama, Jeremy Karmel, take the time to explain the absolute importance of a Fourth Estate (the media) as the most important pillar of our Democratic Republic:
Here is what they say:

"Journalism has long been regarded as an important force in government, so vital to the functioning of a democracy that it has been portrayed as an integral component of democracy itself. In 1841, Thomas Carlyle wrote, "Burke said there were Three Estates in Parliament; but, in the Reporters' Gallery yonder, there sat a Fourth Estate more important far than they all" (On Heroes and Hero Worship).

Four years earlier, Carlyle had used the phrase in his French Revolution: "A Fourth Estate, of Able Editors, springs up, increases and multiplies; irrepressible, incalculable." Carlyle saw the press as instrumental to the birth and growth of democracy, spreading facts and opinions and sparking revolution against tyranny.

"The fact of the matter is that democracy requires informed citizens. No governing body can be expected to operate well without knowledge of the issues on which it is to rule, and rule by the people entails that the people should be informed. In a representative democracy, the role of the press is twofold: it both informs citizens and sets up a feedback loop between the government and voters.

The press makes the actions of the government known to the public, and voters who disapprove of current trends in policy can take corrective action in the next election. Without the press, the feedback loop is broken, and the government is no longer accountable to the people. The press is therefore of the utmost importance in a representative democracy. Today, the press is more concerned with making fake news than with reporting real news, so it will be a tough challenge indeed.

"Another, related, function of the press is to expose people to opinions contrary to their own. This function is perhaps the most valuable in the Internet age; while people can in theory get information about the actions of their government from online sources, it is all too easy to find opinions online that match one's own. Informed decision-making on the part of voters requires an awareness of multiple points of view, which is not likely to be obtained if voters bear the sole responsibility of seeking out information on relevant issues.

The news media provides a forum for debates to take place, as well as moderating and curating the arguments presented by all sides. It is, of course, idealistic to suppose that media give equal, or even proportional, representation to all opinions, but the fact that many media outlets present themselves as nonpartisan sources of information makes them a better forum for debate than online sources such as blogs, which are typically maintained by one individual or a small group of people with similar opinions..."

It would be nice if the mainstream media took the time to provide forums in their media to inform the public of the candidacies of all citizens running in all elections. Even if it were not every day, and the media used its power to permit short speeches to be carried on their on-line sites. The media's job in our Republic is to inform the public and let me just say they can do a far better job than what they do. When you consider that in the three times that I have run for office, the media was mostly MIA, I can say I know from experience.

I have not even been interviewed or permitted to participate in any event on Public Television, even though we the people pay for it. I was interviewed when I ran for Mayor on Election Day but the channel WBRE TV in my home town chose not to run the video. Let me repeat, the media does a disservice to the community by not informing the public of its choices.

I have never been endorsed by any media outlet as I have never been well known by their advertising departments.

Reporters and Newspaper Executives are not easy to move to your side. They do not feel obligated to assure that the public knows what each candidate has to offer.

The Press's problem in this general election season is that "Nobody expects that a guy 'who nobody knows,' will run for office." And so, I know that as a candidate, I will be very close to being summarily ignored.

I do not think that anybody in the Press tries to purposely hurt me or any other candidate, but they have their favorites. From my experience in the past, even after writing letters to the editor and sending multiple press releases trying to assure the media that I am a viable candidate, I found myself excluded from much of the news coverage. Whether it was intentional or not, no media outlet tried to make up for the loss of publicity my campaigns suffered.

I would hope that regardless of how well known a candidate may be in this upcoming election, the papers and the other news media of NEPA should permit candidates to do things that help the people become informed about where they stand on the major issues of the day. In the past, I have had few vehicles provided for me that would help the people know who I am.

Thus, anybody other than an incumbent or one well-endowed by blessings (cash) can expect to be relegated to the back seat in an election.

The papers. TV, and Radio etc. should permit candidates to submit a short essay, perhaps several times during the campaign. In some media, a short essay per week might be appropriate. In others, a mere mention every now and then would be very informative for the people. The local government should also provide areas in which candidates can give speeches...but in my area, they do not.

The charter of the press is to provide news to the people, and news about who may be chosen to represent the people is worthy news indeed.

For me, the bottom line is that it is not easy for democracy to continue when the people have a tough time getting on the ballot and then they must fight against mythical forces to convince even their neighbors that they are serious in the endeavor. My political friends say that is the nature of the beast. I say, the beast is the problem.

Thank you for reading and / or visiting my site:

Chapter 9 Brian Kelly for the US Senate-- Platform

The points in this platform may form the basis for your platform.

Platform -- Influenced by Alan Keyes

In addition to the special platform points displayed in the Brian Kelly announcement speech in the last chapter of this book, and the entire "Make America Great" agenda of President Trump, please examine the following platform points to know more about your candidate.

As Brian was evaluating the items to include in the platform, he used the existing work of Alan Keyes, one of his favorite Americans. This assisted him in quantifying the issues of the American people. The following platform, however, is not that of Alan Keyes. It is Brian Kelly's platform, and as you know, Brian Kelly is hoping to gain your favor as the candidate running in Pennsylvania against Bob Casey for the US Senate from Pennsylvania.

Please read the items well as they are categorized in alphabetic order. The items within the categories are arranged in no significant sequence.

If you have questions or concerns about any of these, feel free to start a forum thread or send Brian an email at bk@kellyfoussenate.com. Thank you for your time and patience.

A. Abortion

1. A child has a God-given right to life from fertilization to natural death.
2. All unborn children are persons, not masses of flesh.
3. Abortion is "prohibited" in Declaration of Independence- prohibit abortion.
4. Embryonic stem cell research experiments with human life.
5. Human embryos in such research "gravely immoral" and unnecessary.
5. Need a Constitutional amendment defining life from conception.
6. Abortion is unjust and immoral.
7. Mothers have no right to take a womb baby's life.
8. Only exception is to preserve life of mother.
9. Brian Kelly is pro mom and pro-baby. No mom feels good after killing a womb baby.
etc.

B. Budget & Economy

1. Deficits must be eliminated.
2. Out-of-control spending must stop.
3. Budget must be balanced just like a household.
4. Balanced budget amendment to the Constitution is a great idea.
5. Need amendment to the Constitution to limit borrowing and spending.
6. No company is too big to fail.
7. If your business can't make it, expect no government help.

8. Government can have no stake in private enterprise (GM etc.).
9. No more bailouts period.
10. Eliminate "pork"
11. Cut Spending -- address the Debt

C. Civil Rights

1. Redefine separation of church & state according to Constitution.
2. Protect religion from the state, but not vice versa.
3. Right to acknowledge God is the foundation of all our rights.
4. Public display of the Ten Commandments is a state's right.
5. Official language of US is English.
6. Marriage is between a man and a woman.
7. Civil unions OK without the notion of or the word, "marriage."

C1. Affirmative Action

8. We cannot cure a past injustice with another injustice.
9. Preferential affirmative action patronizes blacks, women, other "minorities.'
10. Affirmative action is discrimination in reverse.

D. Corporations

1. Corporations should not have citizenship.
2. Corporations should not be permitted to become too big to fail.
3. Corporate mergers do not serve the public well-being.
4. Corporations should have plans to use American workers in America
5. Corporations should pay the social cost of "offshoring" jobs.
6. Corporations want cheap immigrant labor to replace Americans.
7. Corporate executives employing illegal employees should go to jail.
8. Incentives should be given corporations to not engage in labor arbitrage.
9. Workers' pensions need to be separate & protected in bankruptcy
10. Create two tier corporate income tax e.g. 10% domestic, 35% foreign
11. Tax penalty e.g. 20% for offshoring jobs
12. $5.00 per hour tax for each hour of illegal alien work.
13. Reduce foreign visas such as H1-B by 90% to save American jobs.

E. Crime

1. Death penalty is sometimes essential
2. Oppose "hate crimes" legislation -- redundant they are already crimes.
3. Harsh penalties for gang-related crimes in the same vein as RICO.

F. Education

1. Sex education is a private responsibility.
2. This is a Christian Nation.. Prayers to Christ or any god should not be barred.
3. Schools forfeit funds if they expose kids to gay propaganda / pornography.
4. Sex education if it exists at all, should be abstinence-based.
5. Relationship of college tuition rises & taxpayer subsidies is a big problem.
6. Funding for any agency promoting a political entity should be cut--Dept of Education was using taxpayers' dollars to promote the President
7. Teachers keep politics out of classroom -- no political indoctrination
8. Federal government may not use dollar incentives to affect state behavior. All states share equally according to population
9. Common Core -- Out! No Fed influence in education

G. School Choice

1. Parents & local citizens know better than educated masters.
2. Empower parents to choose schools that reflect their values.
3. Break up the government monopoly on public education.
4. Eliminate Department of Education -- use parental / local boards.
5. Pro-voucher; keep fed gov't out of K-12 education.
6. Money should follow parents' education choices.
7. Outlaw politically correct brainwashing.
8. Empower parents against the monopoly of public schools.
9. Let communities decide school rules-- such as all-male / female academies.
19. Make & Female restrooms

H. School Prayer

1. Who allowed the judges to drive God out of our schools?
2. Prohibiting school prayer creates a godless, anything goes society.
3. Christian schooling should receive tax credits. Religion taught off hours
4. Advocate prayer wherever you want in schools
5. God in schools may keep Columbine-like shooters out.

6. Constitution does not forbid prayer in schools.
7. Need prayer in schools and by educators.

I. Energy & Oil & Environment

1. Cap and Trade or similar legislation if enacted, needs to be repealed.
2. Need to seriously develop proper alternative fuels but do not force technology while fossil fuels including coal still work quite well. .
3. Drill here, Drill now in the meantime. Assure off-shore safety
4. Build clean and safe nuclear plants in the meantime.
5. Energy impact of hybrid fuels needs to be evaluated.
6. Ethanol burns more energy than it saves, and it raises food prices?
7. Explore & exploit ANWR, while respecting ecology.
8. Drill Offshore in all states that permit it.
9. "Global Warming is a hoax" so bad name changed to "Climate Change"
10. A Prophet should never make a profit" Al Gore - an approaching green billionaire
11. Against Copenhagen & Kyoto Treaty
12. CAFE standards kill people in crashes - abolish them.

J. Foreign Policy

1. Speak softly but carry a really big stick
2. Use common sense to make trade agreements that benefit U.S.
3. Evaluate the idea of not so free trade
4. Eliminate Trans Pacific (TPP)
5. Gain International concurrence diplomatically but act for the US
6. Recognize the UN as an anti-US agency.

K. Government Reform

1. Amendment for Initiation, Referendum, Recall at Fed level.
2. Give people a voice to overcome legislators' personal opinions.
3. Strictly limit government to the enumerated powers.
4. Focus on moral sovereignty, tax reform, & sealing the border.
5. No union or corporate or foreign donors to campaigns.
6. Disallow lawsuits that stop public officials invoking God.
7. Churches may identify candidates who favor its principles.
8. Congress should have last word, not supreme court
9. People through Initiation and Referendum get the last word.
10. Obeying the dictate of federal judges means no Constitution.

11. Less Government Control
12. Unlimited campaign contributions, but only by people, & well publicized.
13. Panel to examine constitutionality of executive orders
14. Congress can pick unconstitutional EOs without court appearances and eliminate them w/o Pres. concurrence

L. Gun Control

1. Fiercely defend the Second Amendment
2. Fundamental DUTY of free citizens to keep & bear arms.
3. Gun control mentality means crooks have all the guns.
4. Second Amendment not about hunting, but about national duty.
5. No federal role in gun safety-leave it to states & parents.

M. Health Care

1. Repeal all aspects of Obamacare including the "Porkulus" bureaucracy
2. Euthanasia violates unalienable right to life.
3. Patient in charge; no government-controlled health care.
4. No mandated health insurance and universal coverage.
5. Enhanced EMTALA and Enhanced Medicaid
6. Healthcare Accountability / Healthcare Loans
7. Eliminate pre-existing conditions, policy limits for insurance policies.
8. Protect disabled and vulnerable people like Terri Schiavo.
9. Encourage insurance reward for avoiding tobacco, alcohol, obesity.
10. People should take care of their own health.
11. Sensibly cap malpractice awards --- tort reform.
12. Health insurance purchases across state lines to reduce costs
13. Doctor / patient relationship key factor in any change
14. No Medicare cutbacks in treatment or access
15. Market determines health payments, not bureaucrats
16 Govt. becomes advocate for not v people.

N. Homeland Security

1. Peace through strength.
2. Strong & prepared military.
3. Eliminate political correctness from homeland security and the military
4. Assure Homeland Security Director takes mission seriously.
5. Assure Homeland Security Director believes we are at war.
6. Assure Homeland Security Director is competent.

7. Close up the border.
8. Penalize businesses who hire illegals before Americans - $5 tax per hour.
9. Stand unalterably opposed to all who commit terrorist acts.
10. Killing innocents by terror is same evil as by abortion.
11. Protect military chaplains' right to pray in preferred faith.
12. Allow Christian symbols in national war memorials.
      Country was founded as Christian!
13. No student visas to citizens of terrorist states.
14. Coordinate terror watch list with no-fly list
15. Doctrine of terror is killing innocent people.
16. Develop oil independence plan.
17. Drill Here. Drill Now!
18. Don't use Patriot Act to take away freedoms.
19. Send a clear message to the entire terror network.
20. Take preemptive action only if a probable threat exists.
21. Rapidly develop, deploy and/or enhance anti-missile defense systems.
22. Allies share cost of financing terror war efforts.
23. Supports missile strikes against terrorists abroad. (Aug 1998)
24. Establish an effective National Border Guard
25. Seal the borders of the United States

O. Immigration

1. Vigilant maintenance of our sovereign territory and borders.
2. Enforce existing laws against illegal immigration.
3. Sovereignty is betrayed when our borders are not defended.
4. Immigration, yes; colonization, no: oppose guest workers.
5. Control border first, or no other laws matter.
6. Blacks are hurt first by cheap immigrant labor.
7. Excessive multiculturalism weakens American culture.
8. Rescind Bush's order allowing Mexican trucks on US roads.
9. Oppose amnesty
10. Oppose guest workers until unemployment under 5%.
11. Extending privileges to non-citizens invites lawbreaking.
12. Expand orderly legal immigration as appropriate; curtail illegal immigration.
13. No U.S. citizenship for "anchor babies" of non-citizens
14. No immigrants from countries who are controlled of terrorists.
15. Pass something like a Resident Visa Plan and Pay to Go for existing illegals.

P. Jobs

1. Provide tax cuts to small businesses to help them provide real jobs
2. Encourage job creation as means to provide health insurance.
3. Work with corporations to undo damage of offshoring
4. Work with corporations to encourage jobs brought back to US
5. Penalize corporations that are bad citizens re: jobs. gov't contracts, etc.
6. No "sexual orientation" in Employment Non-Discrimination Act.
7. Government does not create jobs, only businesses do.
8. Family farms are nursery of moral character.
9. Create two tier corporate income tax -- 10% domestic, 35% foreign
10. Tax penalty to 20% for offshoring jobs
11. $5.00 per hour tax for each hour of illegal alien work.
12. Reduce foreign visas such as H1-B by 90% to save American jobs.

Q. Social Security & Medicare

1. Keep promises to those who paid so long.
2. Repeal the theft of $700 Billion for Obamacare from Medicare
3. Start Paying Back the SS & Medicare Fund -- generously
4. Tell the truth about COLA and CPI
5. Examine public land and offshore for energy as Social Security and Medicare funding source.
6. Oil companies pay the taxpayers for taking public oil.

R. Tax Reform

1. Repeal the Sixteenth Amendment.
2. Implement Fair Tax
3. Turn off spigot that funds politician's ambitions
4. Income tax has failed. Special people know the loopholes
5. Tax code filled with favors for special interests.
6. Replace income tax with a (1) national sales tax (FAIR Tax)
7. Abolish the income tax and IRS and spend money responsibly
8. National sales tax (Fair Tax) does give control back to people.
9. Augment taxing with tariffs & duties.
10. Income tax gives govt. too much control
11. Excise taxes allow citizens to control tax rate themselves.
12. "Soak the rich" schemes have un-American socialist objectives.

S. Technology

1. No Fairness Doctrine: no equal time if morally objectionable
2. Apply broadcast indecency rules to cable networks
3. Publicly fund NASA
4. Explore space aggressively -- Russia or China in Space is a threat.

T. War & Peace

1. Iraq / Afghanistan -- not best wars -- fight to win or get out
2. Use more technology and less troops.
3. Withdrawing before your enemy stops is called "defeat".
4. Need more countries to share the load
5. Do not go to war frivolously
6. Call Terrorism terrorism and fight it aggressively
7. Do not let Muslim immigrants into US until vetting procedures can be accomplished
8. Defeat ISIS big time by strength and cunning
9. Build areas within Syria & Mideast for returning immigrants to be safe.

U. Welfare & Poverty

1. Constitution does not require separation of church and state.
2. Charity to / from people, not from the government
3. Shift welfare from government to the faith sector.
4. Disintegration of the family causes social ills.
5. Encourage work instead of punishment if one parent goes to work
6. No welfare reward for having a baby.
7. Create a Welfare Accountability System for pay-backs

Use whatever you need from this list of platform items. Start with this list and delete and add as appropriate.

Chapter 10 Brian Kelly Is a JFK Democrat

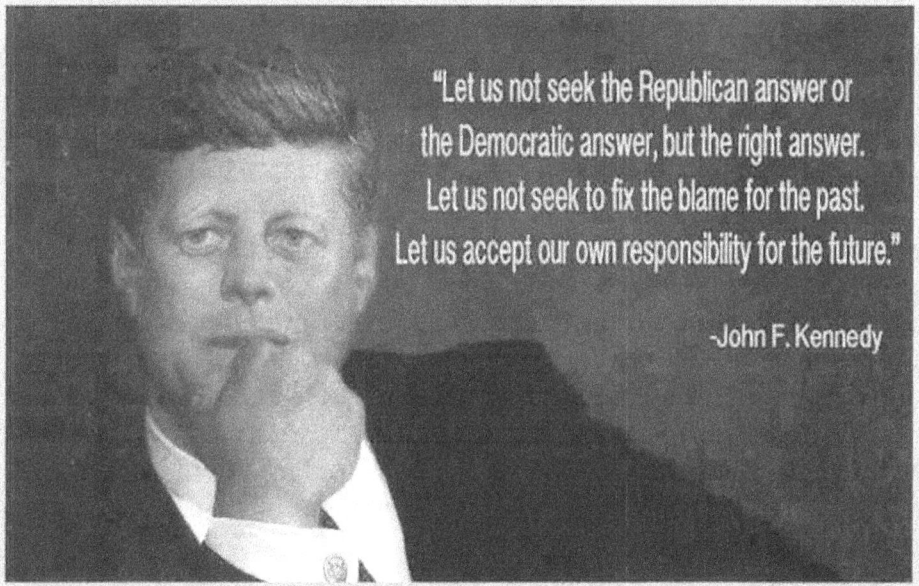

"Let us not seek the Republican answer or the Democratic answer, but the right answer. Let us not seek to fix the blame for the past. Let us accept our own responsibility for the future."

-John F. Kennedy

Feel free to compare yourself and your platform to some well-known and well-liked statesmen that are well-liked by the people.

Being A JFK Democrat

You may wonder why I am a JFK Democrat instead of a conservative Republican? The fact is that neither party is perfect for me. I am for business but not for unbridled corporate power. I am for unions but not for thug tactics in the workplace and I am not for forced unionism.

I worked for IBM for 23 years and at the time, IBM never had nor needed a union. Corporations should treat employees right and unions should be for the employees and not on the same team as the managers. At IBM, the founders believed that if you take care of the people, the people will take care of the business. It worked!

I am pro-life, and I am against selling baby parts and live brains, though some legislators such as say, Bob Casey Jr., the incumbent, forget this. Deep down most Americans are pro-life. Who wants to kill babies when they are the most vulnerable--when they have not made their first goo or gaw?

I do not believe in protecting smelts and trees if it causes harm to human beings. God made human beings with dominion over all life, and though we must be just caretakers of this awesome responsibility, it should not mean that humans must starve or be cold or freeze in the wintertime to please somebody's twisted agenda.

In many ways some of the great ambitions of the Democratic Party leaders to create an equal world where there is no injustice has placed human beings per se in the back seat and has elevated non-humans to a status not intended by God. What good is it to freeze in the winter simply because the EPA has chosen to ban coal? I grew up with a coal stove in my living room and kitchen as did my wife, and we are still healthy. Plus, we (the USA) have plenty of coal for the rest of the world. Why shut off the spigot? Why? It makes no sense. China is killing us economically using coal!

Don't you think that protecting unborn babies is more important than protecting turtle eggs? Since it is a crime to destroy turtle eggs, at a minimum, it should also be a crime to kill an unborn child? Who is not pro baby? I think the big shot elite leaders of the Democratic Party have begun to endorse philosophies that give Government, rather than God, supreme power. I believe that God rules supreme above all else. When was the last time you were at a deathbed and heard the grieving family praying to the government?

Though recently I have come to like the philosophies of populists and conservatives like Marco Rubio and Donald Trump and Ben Carson and Ted Cruz. I am not for communists such as Bernie Sanders nor for wannabe communists such as Hillary Clinton. There is no good choice on the Democrat side. Sorry! JFK is sorely needed!

Like the Republican nominees, I do not think that corporations were meant to dominate individuals. I also think that American corporations have an obligation in exchange for the privilege of operating in America to care for their employees and to help do everything in their power to protect and create American Jobs.

Hiring illegal aliens must be verboten!

Republicans and many rich Democrats even prominent Democrats such as John Kerry and the Heinz Company have no problem taking jobs overseas. Additionally, they have no problem trying to reduce the American wage to as low as possible by bringing in illegal foreign workers to force the wages down.

Neither party wants to enforce our immigration laws. Republicans want lower wages and Democrats see a huge voter pool in those who are granted amnesty. I am for safe and secure borders and I believe in an America for Americans. If foreigners can live legally within our borders according to our laws, I am for that also. But, American citizens, that's us folks, must come first instead of last.

I would like to share with you, information on a site that describes how to be a conservative (JFK) Democrat. My philosophies for the most part fit this description.
http://www.ehow.com/how_2090667_be-conservative-democrat.html

How to Be a Conservative Democrat
Contributor: By eHow Contributing Writer
Article Rating: (11 Ratings)

In politics sometimes, it seems easy to categorize a person by their party affiliation. A Republican is conservative, and a Democrat is liberal. That is too limiting and shortsighted. Party affiliation does not eliminate individual thought. Defying these stereotypes is not always easy but is what democracy is based on--freedom of thought and choice.

Instructions for being a conservative Democrat

1. Step 1
Believe in small government. Small government means limiting the sprawling bureaucracy that invades people's lives and tries to tell them how to live those lives. Small government also means limiting monetary waste in government that comes with oversized government programs.

2. Step 2

Understand that there are services that the government needs to offer. While the conservative Democrat is against big government, they realize that some social programs are necessary for the country to thrive.

3. Step 3

Realize that a strong military force is a good. While curtailing government spending is prudent, it should not be at the expense of the nation's military. Even in times of peace, a strong military can be a deterrent to other aggressive countries and governments.

4. Step 4

Sympathize with the working class. A conservative democrat understands that the working class is the backbone that built this country. Conservative Democrats keep this in mind whenever taking issue with a policy or ideology.

5. Step 5

Focus on education and family values. Education and family values are an important part of the core values of the conservative Democrat. Education is what made this country a world leader and needs to be the focus of a conservative Democrats political agenda.

6. Step 6

Consider free market capitalism a positive endeavor. A conservative Democrat understands that the free market and capitalism empower the individual to make her own destiny.

For Democrats who feel as I do about life, I am clearly your candidate for Pennsylvania, and I would appreciate your vote.

Chapter 11 Mr. Smith Goes to Washington

Use Jimmy Stewart from the movie, Mr. Smith Goes to Washington as a Guide for your campaign. The people like Jimmy Stewart and they like honest guys like Jefferson Smith.

Mr. Smith Goes to Washington

Ladies and Gentlemen, I would like to present myself. My name is Jefferson Smith and I am going to Washington—if you select me of course.

Jimmy Stewart is one of my favorite actors of all time. He is as Americana as it gets with the perfect touch of honesty that makes even men admire the actor and the character the actor is playing. My favorite movie of all time is "It's A Wonderful Life." It gets me every time. Remember the big pot of cash the neighbors brought in to George Bailey, so he could keep the Building and Loan going. Well, that's how I think America should be. Every hard-working American deserves a break.

What George Bailey did not need was the government stealing from his neighbors so that he could go to college and to heck with Pottersville. Well, it would have been Pottersville if George had not stayed to help all the people in Bedford Falls with his dad's Building and Loan Company. Government intervention creates Pottersvilles and good neighbors create the likes of Bedford Falls. Let's let good people be good people again rather than taking so much from them that Mr. Potter is the only one left with any money.

Mr. Smith Goes to Washington exudes the same emotion from the viewer. It was another of Frank Capra's big hits and Jimmy Stewart as Jefferson Smith is as down to earth as George Bailey. I don't propose that I can do as good a job for Northeastern PA as Jefferson Smith did for his constituency. However, I am as much a babe in the woods as far as politics go as Mr. Smith.

I am running for office to help fight the same type of corruption that Smith faced when he went to Washington. I am up to the task and I am ready to fight to make America, America again. There is nothing separating me from my chance other than this general election and your write-in. I thank you very much in advance for the vote.

You may know that Kelly is the second most common family name in Ireland (after Murphy). It is the 69th most popular surname in the United States. Kelly in many ways is like Jones and Smith.

And so, will you indulge me please as I say again. My name is Mr. Smith, and I am going to Washington. I can't get there without your help.

Think of the corrupt conditions that existed in this famous movie as Mr. Smith, played by Jimmy Stewart. Smith was little more than a bumpkin, when he first went into the Washington swamp of iniquity. For Smith, it was the US Senate. He was the naive and idealistic Jefferson Smith, the leader of the Boy Rangers. In Washington, Smith soon discovers many of the shortcomings of the political process as his earnest goal of a national boys' camp leads to a conflict with the state's corrupt political boss, Jim Taylor.

Taylor first tries to corrupt Smith and then later attempts to destroy Smith through a made-up scandal. Smith conducts a filibuster and finally sways everybody to not pass the healthcare bill. Wouldn't that be nice! (It was the Boy Rangers Bill). Smith would be working to get the bill repealed if it were passed, and the movie would have taken a bit longer. Kelly will make the repeal of the 2700 page bill a priority and will replace it with an EMTALA-like bill in the neighborhood of 4 to 8 pages. Additionally, Brian has a great plan for illegal interlopers and he will wipe out all student debt now and Boost Social Security so that the elderly can keep living in their homesteads.

Stranger things have happened. I hope to be like your Mr. Smith if you select me. And, so, I ask you to send me to Washington to serve in the United States Senate instead of Bob Casey. I hope there are approximately 32 additional like-thinking Senators sworn in when I have the honor to take office in January 2019. I want to thank you all. Thank you very much.

Chapter 12 Americans Are in Revolt

Remember in your campaign that countervailing power is good power.

Countervailing power is the only solution!

Those with power sometimes do not know how powerful they are while those without power know very well how weak they are. The have's always have and the have-nots, have not ever--but they do their best to survive. So, it has been from the beginning of time as the major law of the universe dictates: "survival of the fittest."

Are humans above it all? Is there just a little bit in a human that is animal? Is it possible that part really is not as good in its spirit as man's best friend, the wonderful creature called dog? Are humans or dogs more inclined to do the right thing if called upon accordingly? Tough question!

I look into my wonderful dog's eyes and I know which way he is going to go. When I look a human in the eye, it is my history with the person more than the look in his eye that matters. But, the look in his eye does matter. I admit that it is good to have a fine canine friend help out in the evaluation. Who is good; and who is bad? Dogs seem to know!

As we go back to the turn of the 20th century we find certain humans who had lots and lots of material goods as well as lots of power. These folks were truly captains of industry and they were referred to as "Robber Barons." That term was not very flattering to these people who went to church each week in fine clothes, hoping to charm even the priests into believing in their goodness. But, there was little goodness there!

Robber Barons was not a very flattering term for anybody at the time and it is not a well-appreciated term today. It implies that certain Barons are robbers. They rob the people. We all know who they are and who they were in real times from our unedited American History classes. John D. Rockefeller, Milton S. Hershey, J.P. Morgan, Andrew Carnegie, and Cornelius Vanderbilt were the headliner robber barons of the period. They were all shrewd, cunning, and some might add heartless businessmen of the period. Even they may not have known they were so bad. .

These Robber Barons were indeed captains of industry and they were indeed, robber barons.

They had immense power and ran huge companies and hired many people to work in their facilities. For the workers, it was good because they had a job and they were able to provide for their families, though just barely. For the families, it was not so good because the head of the household had to work most of his waking hours every day of the week. The Robber Barons believed, perhaps even sincerely, that they were providing a modicum of wealth for the plebeians of the new America.

There is a very offensive term that has been used for some time to describe one of the worst acts of the Robber Barons. This term is "labor arbitrage." It came from this period of American History as the Robber Barons tried their best to assure that the wage they paid was the absolute minimal wage. And, they did pay only as much as legally required.

Only the Robber Barons held the power in the period before and immediately after the turn of the twentieth century. The irony is that the workers did not really understand their value in the wealth creation process. The workers were the means to the Barons' wealth. Yet, they had no power, and in most cases were living in destitute circumstances.

The worker had power but could not realize it individually. This enabled the barons to exact upon the workers whatever terms were favorable to the barons alone. The workers were mere resources. Though they were clearly the means to the barons' wealth, nobody on the Robber Baron team was about to reveal this to them.

In the power game, the barons had all the power and the workers had none. -- zero, nada, zilch as they like to say today. Thus, there was a power void. Whenever there is a power void, it will eventually be filled as the seemingly powerless realize that in numbers, they have power. In the days of the Robber Barons, the barons were able to essentially enslave the workers because there was no notion of a countervailing power, and no means of achieving it even if the notion were well known.

What is countervailing power and why is it important?

Wikipedia authors often get it right, "Modern economies give massive powers to large business corporations to bias this process, and there arise 'countervailing' powers in the form of trade unions, citizens' organizations and so on, to offset business's excessive advantage."

Corporations at the turn of the century were just becoming legal and powerful and this was coincident with the Robber Baron period. Corporations were like little dictatorships that created worker cities ruled mostly by tyrants all within the democracy of the United States. This was not a proud moment in American History.

The greed exhibited by one corporation during this period forced another corporation to be as greedy as the first or go out of business. So, corporations and the men (at the time) who ran them, chose to be as greedy as they could be. They viewed it as much a matter of survival as a means to success.

The conditions were perfect. There was a large supply of labor and many needy families willing to send any member into the factory. This set the stage for the ultimate labor arbitrage. So, let's examine this notion of labor arbitrage in light of countervailing power. Quite simply, Labor arbitrage is the movement of the wage which industry must pay for workers to the lowest possible level.

Labor arbitrage creates big hurts in lots of regular people. In many ways in 2016, the "new immigrants," undocumented workers," "illegal foreign nationals," or quite simply, "illegal aliens, are driving American wages down again to the point of labor arbitrage, and it is not by accident.

The Robber Barons are documented as having exploited Americans, using sweatshops with abysmally low wages. They were fully in control of the labor arbitrage. If workers had to work just 10 hours a day, it was an easy shop but sometimes the periods included 18-hour work shifts, without overtime pay. The abuses of the period included child labor; inadequate safety, minimal health and environmental safeguards; and of course, no pension or health benefits--for most Americans.

There seemed to be no escape. If a worker of that era tried to change his plight, he might be summarily discharged for union organizing. There were a lot of reasons for families to just accept their condition as it was dealt. The Robber Barons assured that those who accepted their dire circumstances were able to survive, though in the most meager ways.

Humans are animals and when animals are pinched and hurt, and their young are hurting, life is different than when you and I are screaming at the TV set because of things as trite as that our favorite team did not score. If the team is Notre Dame, and if I (Brian Kelly) were the coach, then perhaps the screaming would be appropriate and responsible. But, that again is not the theme of this chapter.

Eventually, when you are really hurting, finding a solution because of the gravity of a problem such as labor arbitrage with no countervailing power is far more important than the fear of repercussions. A solution must come one way or another. From every void a solution will come.

At the turn of the last century, however, there was a huge void. People were hurting, and it seemed they were helpless. However, every now and then, brave men would come by to help. These were union organizers and they tried their best to fill the void. The union organizers intrinsically knew that giving power to the worker was the only solution to labor arbitrage.

Yet, employees knew that the best they could do would be to be able to barely make it if they made no waves at all. If they made some waves, such as fraternizing with a labor organizer, they might be left with nothing. The choice to organize was difficult as the risks were high.

The union workers were very brave souls with a real mission. They suffered, and all suffered when trying to take the smallest action to avoid the tyranny of the Robber Barons. Can you imagine working for the Baron and trying to overcome the Baron at the same time?

There is an idea that if a decent wage were paid to the workers-- not substantially larger but seemingly generous, the Robber Barons would have been able to keep their gold and the worker would have achieved the opportunity to live more hours per week with family, rather than at the factory. But, with no countervailing power, the Robber Barons were more concerned about competing against other Robber Barons. They had no regard at all for the power of the worker who was merely part of the means of production. The worker simply had no power.

Wherever and whenever there is a power void, it will be filled.

Over time, unions developed strategies to face and to compete against the all-powerful captains of industry, the Robber Barons. They demanded better wages and better benefits for workers. The unions became the countervailing power against the Robber Barons / corporations that had been missing from the foray for far too long.

Soon after unions were integrated into the fabric of America, life got better for everybody -- workers and even the former barons. Though the sins of the Robber Barons were hard to forgive, the unions helped them to stop sinning against their fellow human-kind.

Enter the Politician

Political corruption is not new to our times. When the Robber Barons had the wealth, there were plenty of politicians who favored their way of life and benefited from it immensely. The people did not count. The political process has not changed much, unfortunately.

When the unions gained power, and perhaps as a means of that power, there were politicians who recognized the winds of change and prepared to accept their largesse from Unions as there had come a choice.

Once the countervailing power had been duly established, neither corporations nor unions controlled the scenario. Both were very powerful, and the unions did their best for the worker while the corporation did its best for the former baron class citizens.

Eventually both the corporations and the unions noticed that there was a very large and available third party that had entered the ring. Actually, it had always been there but in the early days it represented only we the people. The third party was actually to have been the "people" as represented by the Congress, the Senate, the President, and the Supreme Court. Instead, the third party in its public face was just the government with all of its inelegant bureaucracy.

Of course, when it chose to do so, and only when it was inclined, this third party known as the government, did claim to represent ordinary people. However, most of the time, as we have all come to realize in 2018, the temptation of the politician to feed himself from the public troth is so overwhelming that he has little time to include we the people in his greed-driven thought process. Self-serving politicians are more visible today because they promise the people everything to get elected.

John Quinton called it right when he described the greed of a politician in this way: "Politicians are people who, when they see light at the end of the tunnel, go out and buy some more tunnel."

The corporations and the unions fought for the control of this powerful entity known as the government. Whoever won over the politician had the tie breaker on their side. For the most part, only at election time did the people matter. And, we know politicians love their perquisites. Depending on which politician was on-the-take or as they would like to have it said, "depending on which group got the politician's ear," things moved in that direction with a little help from government friends.

Does that sound like today? Does that sound like Bob Casey's US Senate? Why did Bob Casey Jr. not vote to reduce the tax burden on Americans? He'll tell you that Nancy Pelosi and Chuck Schumer told him to vote against putting more in Americans' pockets because the crumbs were not worth it. Yet, today's Americans have grown accustomed to the thousands of dollars in "crumbs" they otherwise would never have been able to spend.

None of my Democrat friends want to give back two or three thousand a year or more to the government? Remember this. Bob Casey Jr. thinks that you do. He thinks you do not need extra money. Brian Kelly thinks you enjoy every dime you get to spend even if someone else calls them crumbs. Elect Bob Casey and the crumbs and the thousands of dollars will go away. Elect Brian Kelly and the thousands you have will multiply and the rest of the country will also prosper.

God bless you all.

One Last Thought!

There is some good news. People are beginning to think that things are out of control and perhaps the countervailing power will have to be some type of internal revolt that helps even things out again.

Mark Thoma had some time on Tuesday, May 15, 2012 at 12:15 AM while sitting in an airline seat and so he posted this great little perspective piece in Economics, Fiscal Policy, and Politics. I have included this short post below and several appropriate comments. He titled his piece as follows:

The Need for Countervailing Power

http://economistsview.typepad.com/economistsview/2012/05/the-need-for-countervailing-power.html

(Though it won't post until later, I may as well try to do something while I sit in this airplane seat.)

Like Brad DeLong, before the recession started I could not have imagined that policymakers would fail to put the unemployed first and foremost in all policy decisions. I was sure the unemployed would come before inflation, before banks, before debt reduction and contrived fights over the debt ceiling. How could we possibly turn our backs on millions of struggling households, especially when doing so creates so many additional long-run problems for individual households and for the economy as a whole? Nothing else would be more important than putting people back to work, and we would, of course, come together and mobilize in a national war against high unemployment.

But I forgot something. With the decline in unions in recent decades, the working class has lost both economic and political power. And at the same time, those at the top end of the income scale have gained power both relatively and absolutely. So why would I have ever thought that the unemployed would come first when they have so little organized political power? Is it any surprise that policy has paid most attention to the issues that just happen to be the things those with the most political power care the most about? What was I thinking?

I suppose I was thinking that politicians were honorable, that money wouldn't trump principle. Silly me. In any case, the question is how to change the balance of power. We could get the money out of politics, but that will never be fully possible. Even with the best of effort, loopholes, bypasses, and the like will always be sought out, found, and exploited too circumvent the rules. That doesn't mean we shouldn't try -- whatever constraints can be imposed are helpful -- but this probably isn't the full answer. We could hope for better politicians, people who represent everyone equally, including the powerless, but I'm certainly not going to count on that either. Finally, we could try to provide (or at least not discourage) a countervailing force, something that replaces the role that unions played for the working class.

I'm not completely sure what form this institution should take, workers lack both economic power in wage negotiations and political power to shape legislation in their favor, or how it could happen short of fed up workers finally demanding change. But workers need to have their interests better represented, and the need for a new institution of some sort is clear.

Comments:

dilbert dogbert said in reply to reason...
When union members are unemployed the union will advocate for them. The union will of course focus its efforts on union members first and foremost. Just like CEO's focus first and foremost on their bonuses.

Min said in reply ...
"The best explanation for this that I can see is that Capital and the bourgeoisie has globalized while the proletariat remains fundamentally national."
Workers of the world, unite!

christy said...
What is needed is a "consumer union".
A consumer union could exercise power by refusing to buy the goods and services of corporations in certain limited circumstances.
Furthermore, the union could gain members by exercising market power and negotiating price reductions for members.

Such a union could be very effective as against, for example, pharmaceutical companies that abuse the patent system by encouraging members to buy competing products across that company's entire product range.
Modern social media would make the organization of such a union very easy indeed.

And all that would be required form members would be a willingness to refrain from buying certain products when requested.
If well-organized such an organization could be effective - its market power would also benefit from network effects and increasing returns form scale

---

And, so, it is what it is! Remember that a write-in vote is an exercise in countervailing power.

Chapter 13 Unique Characteristics of Brian Kelly's US Senate Platform

Note from your author and Senate Candidate Brian W. Kelly

Brian Kelly Chief Technology Officer College Misericordia circa 1994

No, I don't look like this anymore, but I did look like this when as the chief technology officer at College Misericordia in the 1990's, I began to pay a lot more attention to what goes on in our government. The College paid for this picture.

By now, I admit that I am not too happy with what I discovered about government and politics in our country. That, and because like you, I could not afford a full-bore Senatorial campaign, is why I am running as a write-in candidate for the US Senate.

Ask yourself this question: Would you hire any Congressman in America today to run your business—even to babysit your kids? Me neither! Yet, we hire them through the electoral process to run the most complex country that ever was—the United States of America. It is clear that at some point we must begin to make better choices. Why not start in 2018?

I think the best way to begin this book is to give you the announcement speech that I will give the first time I am given a forum in a cost-free venue. There is a lot in this speech but then again, there are many issues today in America. As I review the contents of this speech below, I wish that I could make the speech shorter and at the same time more comprehensive, so you fully know what the platform is all about and why it is worthy of your consideration. I have done my best, but I do admit that this is not one of my shortest speeches. Thank you.

Originally, I wrote this speech for Congressman Lou Barletta, hoping he would adopt the platform elements in this speech as his own. I believe the Congressman likes these ideas but as he is running for Senator as a Republican, it would be difficult to convincing officials in the Republican Party of their worth. It would be tough to push a platform that may have a negative effect on the budget cuts Republicans are seeking. And, so, I decided to go it alone, and instead of expecting the man who I believe may still become Senator Barletta present these ideas for America, I will do the job myself under my own write-in candidacy.

Yet, please, if you must vote Democrat in this election, remember that unlike Bob Casey Jr., I am not a Chuck Schumer or Nancy Pelosi Democrat nor am I a Maxine Watters Democrat nor do I stand for any principle such as the abolishment of ICE that harms the country I love. I would be pleased to accept your vote of confidence for my candidacy. Just write me in.

B-R-I-A-N   K-E-L-L-Y

Don't type the dashes.

Campaign Update August 3, 2018

This is the day after the Donald Trump Rally in Wilkes-Barre, my home town, on behalf of Republican Lou Barletta for the US Senate. As a result of that 1 hour and sixteen-minute rally, Donald Trump's phenomenal speech, his endorsement of Lou Barletta, and an equally great and inspiring speech by Senate Candidate Lou Barletta, I have decided to endorse Congressman Lou Barletta for the US Senate. I am as much **opposed** to Senator Robert 'Sleepin Bob' Casey as I am **in favor** of a great American, Lou Barletta, a man who shares most of my values.

For those Democrats who historically will not vote for a Republican under any circumstances, or those Democrats desiring the package of unique pro-American legislation that I have developed in the past, I encourage you to make a better choice for the US Senate than Bob Casey. Pennsylvania needs a great US Senator. Casey has not been that man and his concern for the people is getting worse, not better. Lou Barletta is the best choice. However, if you must vote Democrat, remember that Bob Casey is not for the people of Pennsylvania. Rather than vote for Casey, you may feel free to write my name in for United States Senator B-R-I-A-N   K-E-L-L-Y. I am a registered Democrat. Thank you.

At the PA Wilkes-Barre Rally, President Trump and Congressman Barletta netted out the same negative case against Bob Casey, Jr as a legislator. Trump began by saying the younger Casey was boring, a nobody in Washington who does what Democratic leaders tell him. I don't think I ever met him, Trump said. Bob Casey is for open borders, Trump asserted, again raising the specter of violent immigrants from Central America overrunning the country.

Barletta and Trump noted that Casey is a pro-abortion, anti-second amendment socialist by his record and he expects Casey to be calling for the abolition of the Immigration and Customs Enforcement (ICE) agency, a favorite cause on the left. He more or less said that Chuck Schumer says "Jump," and Bob Casey says: "How high?" Then, every, time, he goes ahead and jumps. Though Casey says he is not anti-ICE, he also says he is anti-abortion and then votes pro-abortion in almost all cases, such as his opposition to Judges Gorsich and Cavanaugh. For twelve years, Bob Casey Jr. has been the epitome of a do-nothing politician, choosing not to do the people's business. It is time for Casey to make a graceful exit.

Like me, Lou Barletta is for the entire Trump agenda, especially the Wall, and that will be good for America. The only thing that we disagree on is a detailed solution that I put together in several books this year that squarely address resident illegal foreign nationals, Fair COLAs for Seniors, and a major economic stimulus by solving the student loan crisis.

End of Campaign Update

God bless you all and I hope you enjoy my speech. It is so right on for today that I enjoy it every time I read or edit it. Here it is:

Fellow Citizens,

Language is inadequate to express my gratitude for the privilege of submitting before you my candidacy to represent the fine people of Pennsylvania as your US Senator.

I would also like to thank you for the fine welcome, which you all have extended to me on this occasion. As I look out in my mind's eye, I see a vast sea of human faces who share a common interest, as do I, about the greatest questions of our times. Beyond occasionally agitating the mind, they now dominate the concerns of all Pennsylvanians and U.S. citizens, underlying the foundations of our free institutions. Let us all make sure that freedom never becomes just another word for nothing left to lose.

The reaction of my U.S. Senate candidacy by the people of Pennsylvania has been quite heartening. We have a president whose interest quite simply is to "Make America Great Again." By contrast, the embedded establishment and liberal leftovers in the SWAMP, have no interest in performing what is good for our country. They are doing their best to undermine our president, without any repercussions, aided and abetted by a corrupt media, instead of building bridges to work for the good of all Americans.

It is no longer acceptable for a Democrat or a Republican to be a Never-Trumper. Donald Trump is our president and his platform is my platform and when elected, I hope the extras in my platform that I introduce in this speech, become part of the Trump platform.

We all know that "Never-Trumpers" will never hold office again. Democrats such as Bob Casey Jr., my opponent, simply adore the establishment's impediments to the president's agenda with a media whose interests are as adverse to the American people as the British press was during Colonial Times.

The Democrats and the Republican Never-Trumpers in the Senate, House, and the federal bureaucracy and the degenerate mainstream press have done everything they can to thwart the will of 62,979,636 people who voted to clean out the SWAMP with a fresh new presidential administration.

The legendarily venal Hillary Clinton lost the election after the public saw through her charade; yet she continues to parade around the world blaming everything from her own adoring fans at The New York Times, to white women like her, to the DNC, and probably even the cows in Wisconsin, a state she famously lost after taking it so for granted, she never visited.

She even blames the FBI and it never occurs to anyone that the best way to avoid an untimely FBI intervention in a political campaign is to *not run for President while under federal criminal investigation*. And all the while, Senator Casey stood by submissively, applauding and enabling this farce of a candidacy. It is time for the country to move on. She lost, now get over it. We've had twelve years of Casey and that's about as much as any man or woman in America can stand.

I am running for the US Senate to reclaim this seat which rightfully belongs to its people, not the extrinsic interests controlling our politicians who would tear the Constitution in half without hesitation if it would please their donors and cheerleaders in the mainstream media. Despite the shameless lack of virtue that defines the top echelons of our government, our country itself is replete with honest citizens who would be humbled to work on behalf of their fellow countrymen and women. That is why I am running for the US Senate against one of the biggest icons of mainstream mediocrity and corruption, Mr. Bob Casey Jr.

Casey Jr. caters only to the whining anti-Trump crowd who wants to turn every trivial post on Facebook into a new Cuban Missile Crisis. Despite the voters in even his home state rejecting the rank duplicity of former Secretary Clinton and her bleak vision of hopelessness and sovereign state decline, Senator Casey never lifted a finger to help the people who support our president, despite the fact that we outnumber the opposition right here in Pennsylvania. But to him-- that's Bob Casey, folks; we do not even exist.

The Bob Casey Jr. that we all see is a do-nothing Senator who would prefer to turn the US into a globalist abyss rather than support its sovereignty or its people's dignity. Meanwhile, our great president is trying to find everybody a high-paying job by making it easier to conduct business in our country. I intend to help President Trump protect us from such parasitic interests.

If there is one principle most cherished in all free governments, it is that which asserts the exclusive right of a free people to form and adopt their own fundamental laws, to manage and regulate their own internal affairs and domestic institutions. That is under constant attack by Mr. Casey and his legions of Clinton dead-enders.

Electing representatives of the people is not a triviality, but rather the expression of the most fundamental right of self-government. Without it, of course, this great United States would be like any other country in the world. It would not be the exceptional republic, which we the people have enjoyed since our own Declaration of Independence.

To say that I am honored to be here today presenting my candidacy for the US Senate, would be the understatement of the ages. Thank you for your reception and hospitality. I assure you that if elected, I will provide Pennsylvania and the United States of America the best representation in the US Senate of which I am capable. You can be sure of that.

We have many issues today of which the people are concerned. My plan in this address is to limit discussion to just four of the most prominent. My candidacy uniquely addresses each of the four as no other candidate for any US office has ever been able to do. I hope you will find the elements of my platform a welcome refreshment and inclusive of precepts that we all embrace and recognize as sincere and necessary.

My format will be to be present each issue by area of concern and then offer the specific solution which is part of my unique platform. The issues and solutions will be presented one by one in the following four topical areas:

#1—Obamacare.

#2—Illegal Immigration.

#3—Student Debt Crisis Wipe Out All Student Debt Now!

#4—Social Security's Cost-of-Living Fraud – Boost
    Social Security Now!

My pledge is to put forth legislation when elected to help address all four issues. Let's discuss them one by one, starting with Obamacare.

Obamacare

The first problem on the list is #1 because over 54% of Americans say that the availability and affordability of healthcare is their #1 issue. Despite Obama's empty promises, many of us cannot keep our favorite doctors nor can we retain an affordable health plan that meets our needs. The costs have been so prohibitive that many Americans have forestalled doctor's visits with often grave consequences. We all know that despite what Bob Casey would offer you, Obamacare is a disaster.

My solution to Obamacare begins with clarity and definitive purpose. We start with a one-line repeal. The beast is vanquished. Following the repeal, we envision a plethora of competing less expensive alternatives provided by the marketplace without current tyrannical government controls.

Illegal Immigration

In February 2004, Arizona Senator John McCain recognized via Border Patrol reports that nearly four million people crossed our borders "illegally" each year following the Reagan amnesty in 1986. Nonetheless, the fraudulent press insists that the total count of illegal immigrants residing in the United States is eleven million, a mathematical impossibility if Border Patrol figures are to be believed. And of these millions of foreigners, countless amounts receive welfare while, contrary to popular mythology, very few actually work in agriculture.

There may be as many as 60 million and perhaps more illegal foreign nationals living in the United States today. While some individuals in this group may contribute to our society, on balance this is outweighed by the group's overall negative effect on our resources, whether they be drained by government assistance, lost employment opportunities for American citizens, or criminal offenses. It is amazing how effective the fake-ID business is in turning illegal aliens into fake citizens who are thus enabled to enjoy American rights and privileges.

According to the 2011 GAO report entitled "Criminal Alien Statistics," the cost of crimes by illegal foreign nationals is $8.1 billion per year, and that's without even considering the incomprehensibly larger emotional toll this takes on families whose priceless loved ones can never be replaced.

If elected, I will introduce two pieces of legislation that will solve this problem of illegal residents in the shadows once and for all. Besides many other benefits, it stands to save the U.S. over $1 Trillion per year in addition to major reductions in crime. The two solutions are known as pay-to-go and the resident visa program.

Pay-to-Go

It costs taxpayers $30,000 per year on the average, per illegal alien in America. Each illegal resident and their dependent children, who signs up for Pay to Go, on the way back to the home country, will receive a one-time $20,000 stipend plus the individual expense back to the home country. With a cost of $30,000 per year to support unwelcome interlopers, the taxpayer savings begins year one and continues at $30,000 per year forever. Not a bad deal for Americans.

The program therefore quietly accommodates family reunification in the home country. A family of five for example, could do quite well back home after receiving $100,000 in stipends from Uncle Sam. Reuniting families in their own countries is a good idea for them and for America. The savings in welfare means there is no cost in year one and in year 2, the savings equal $30,000 for each person who "goes." back home, never to return.

Resident Visa

Those who do not want to leave the US can sign up, be vetted, and eventually be approved for the Resident Visa. The visa will cost $200.00 to cover vetting in year one and it will be renewable every year thereafter for $100.00 To get a Resident Visa, a former interloper would agree to all stipulations after registering. Stipulations would include full initial vetting; onsite renewal vetting; keep existing jobs; new jobs for Americans first; no voting; no citizenship; no welfare and no freebies of any kind. Everybody is not automatically approved. After vetting, those not approved for the resident visa program may use the Pay-to-Go program to aid in their relocation.

As the program would entail 100% participation from illegal residents, estimates are as high as $500 billion per year cost savings in total for those who choose to go or for those who choose to stay using the no-welfare resident visa. Another $500 billion will be reclaimed over time for lost wages. Additionally, if we can figure a way for countries to reclaim their criminals, there is another $8.1 billion to be recovered.

Once the program is in effect, there would be no more illegal aliens in the country. Resident Visa holders would be legal and so there would be no shadows. There would be no need for DACA and no need for Sanctuary cities Let me repeat that. All issues with DACA would be over and Sanctuary Cities would be a thing of the past because there would be no shadows and no illegal interlopers.

Two additional programs are the part of my platform that I would now like to introduce. Like the resident alien plans, no other candidate for public office includes these great programs in their platform. You are going to love these.

These two new programs offer the promise of a positive effect on the health of the economy and both will contribute to improving it for American citizens of all ages to live well in this country. The first is about wiping out all student debt and the second is about offering Social Security recipients increased benefits to make up for fraudulent cost of living increases based on an intentionally fraudulent consumer price index.

Student Debt is Huge

If we look at the $1.48 Trillion dollars in student loan debt that more and more young adults simply cannot repay, some have asked: "Why do our young people no longer matter?" Do they matter?

We live in an age when everybody seems to have a reason to pick on millennials. They would not loan a "spoiled" millennial "ingrate" as much as a dollar for a cup of coffee.

Whether millennials are deserving of the bad rap or not, they represent a lost generation of our society. For the sake of all of America, they need to be invited back in. We all have student loan debtors in our families – sons, daughters, nephews, nieces, even grandparents and parents when we consider cosigners.

I plan to offer legislation when first elected to make sure we solve this nasty American problem. There have been many other debt reliefs in our history but none that could deliver such an immediate benefit to so many actual Americans all at once. The upside would be overwhelming, a joint humanitarian return and a major economic return far greater than any bailout in history. Let's consider.

A Bailout is a Bailout?

Many of us remember bailouts of the past from 2007 onward. We had bank bailouts, auto company bailouts, TARP bailouts and many other unnamed bailouts. Did any of these help your family? Of course not. Bailout fever began right before Obama became President and continued. The President managed all of the money—trillions. He chose not to give a dime to help student loan debt but spared no expense showering the degenerate financial institutions that owned his candidacy with gold.

Mike Collins, a Forbes Magazine contributor whose expertise focuses on manufacturing and government policy (not the former beloved magistrate of Wilkes-Barre who shares the same name) had this to say:

"Most people think that the big bank bailout was the $700 billion that the treasury department used to save the banks during the financial crash in September of 2008. But this is a long way from the truth because the bailout [ten years later] is still ongoing.

The Special Inspector General for TARP's summary of the bailout says that the total commitment of government is $16.8 trillion dollars with the $4.6 trillion already paid out. The [same] banks are now larger and still too big to fail. But it isn't just the government bailout money that tells the story of the bailout. This is a story about lies, cheating, and a multi-faceted corruption, which was often criminal."

Like most elements of his presidency, Obama made the situation worse when he commandeered the student loans from Sallie Mae and other lenders. The government now pulls in more than $50 billion a year from charging high interest rates to student borrowers. The Obama Student Loan Company charged 6.8% as a student interest rates. The CBO estimates that the interest rate on these loans could quickly be reduced from 6.8 percent to 5.3 percent if Obama had not earmarked the profit from the backs of students to subsidize Obamacare.

Not only were millennials duped into huge college loans when they were so young that Clearasil was one of their major expenses, they were duped into believing Obama was in their corner.

I believe these student victims deserve a break. They are now adults. Some stuck with huge cosign tabs are grandparents on Social security. The government actually garnishes their SSR to pay back the Obama loans.

The federal government is putting up $16.8 trillion dollars as of 2018 to big banks, and other nameless faces receiving bailouts. We still do not know who is getting our money. Yet students who are still being victimized by usury were preyed on as 17-year- olds by admissions counsellors for an all-but worthless college education leading to no job. If given the choice would you be helping the big banks or our own kids?

What do the people think about Student Debt?

Four in ten Americans believe that President Trump's administration should forgive all federal student debt in order to help stimulate the economy, according to a reasonably new survey revealed in 2017. As time goes by as more Americans realize we are excluding a full generation of Americans in our economy, this number will increase from a simple majority to an overwhelming endorsement of wiping out this scurrilous unfair debt as soon as possible. We should bring these 48 million students back into the American way of life as soon as possible.

The largest share blame for the student debt crisis lies with the promises made by over-zealous admissions counsellors convincing kids to sign up for $100,000 loans. No American can want a full generation of other Americans to be left behind in the Trump economy. We need this debt eradicated now and to install safeguards so that seventeen-year-olds in the future are never asked again to sign up for a life in debtor's prison.

According to MoneyTips.com, attitudes have changed from a time when Americans thought college students should be punished for making bad choices to today, when we could use 48 million new spenders in our economy. They would be unleashed into a world of productivity if no longer burdened with massive debt. Many of us know first-hand the consequences of this debt burden. Though millennials may not be the most gracious in asking for help, they are Americans, not DACA immigrants, and they need our help now.

The raw economic fact regardless of your philosophical preference is that spenders with the greatest potential to spend today are not spending at all in real numbers because of student debt. They are not getting married. They are not having families and they are not buying homes. We must solve this scourge on our country so that this generation can produce other generations of Americans.

Our children are not MS-13 members in disguise; there are our kids. American kids. They were snookered to join academia for what they were deceived into believing was an indispensable college degree by depraved loan sharks. Let's give them a full chance. It costs a university nothing when their students with huge loans fail. Please let that sink in.

Let me review the plight of young American college attendees and graduates. Barely out of adolescence, these young Americans were wheedled into commitments based on fraudulent promises by admissions counselors and financial institutions. It was unfair to pit experienced loan sharks against adolescent teenagers. The students were further damned by a paid-for Congress, whose lobbyists insisted that these select few with student debt, distinct from all of the others in America, had no opportunity for any relief in the bankruptcy courts.

Non-college graduates with a trillion dollars in credit card debt are still able to obtain full relief from the courts. Why did Congress exclude these former teenagers, who clearly have been the biggest victims of loan-sharking organized racketeering ever seen in America? Why?

I am pledging today to solve this problem as soon as I can. I am ready to take action. I hope you all agree. Let's help these young Americans before they are lost forever.

Young teenagers were told all through high school that the best ticket for a successful life is a college education. Is this true today? Their salaries often lag behind even those of non-college educated professionals such as plumbers, electricians, computer repair personnel, operating engineers, and more. Because of their reliance on these deliberately false misrepresentations, they now owe an approximate average of $50,000 in student debt while their admissions counsellors and loan sharks revel in riches, in their Mercedes, BMW's, and third vacation home on the lake.

Unscrupulous malefactors with self-interested agendas persuaded America's teenagers, many so young they still had Acne vulgaris, to dig themselves huge financial holes with no escape. Universities are at least partly responsible for their unfulfilled promises. Don't you think? We must also consider what liability they may share in compensating this lost generation where one out of six student borrowers must default today, a figure that only increases with time.

Removing this debt may not fully compensate for the bad hand they were dealt, but its consequent increase in economic activity will benefit all of us. It will boost the US economy beyond expectations. We are already giving bailouts of $17 billion to obscenely rich people in corporate shadows. Right now, we need a mere 10% of that to pay for the write-off of student debt without hurting taxpayers and without putting any banks under. The savings over three years, for example from the resident visa program alone pays off all the student debt that exists today. Why support illegal aliens when we can help Americans?

One last point. It helps to recall that President Obama increased the National Debt by $9.1 Trillion in just eight years, hoping to assure that illegal aliens had all the resources they needed to take as many American jobs as they could. This is six times the amount of debt owed by young Americans. Obama nearly doubled our debt. And what do we have to show for that? As is typical for the Obama years, the answer is frankly... nothing. By contrast, debt relief for our young Americans will be *visibly* positive in its impact.

So, let's say Congress wipes out all student debt because it is the fair thing to do. How do we prevent this from every happening again? For this, I thank my great friend, Dennis Grimes whose solution combines some skin in the game for Academic Institutions to the mix and thus assures that no student will ever carry debt unless the student is successful with a job in their field of study. Here is how the new loan system would work.

Nobody gets a loan unless the college or university agrees to take all of the risk of the loan. If the student is successful, she or he will pay reasonable amounts on a monthly basis. If the student is jobless, since the university vouched for the student, the school will owe all of the debt. Academic institutions are smart. They will stop lending quickly to students with very little prospects of being able to pay the loan back. If students do not maintain acceptable averages, they will be expelled, and the university will pay their balance. If they want to go to college in the future, it will be cash only. What do you think?

A Rigged System

I am confident that President Trump would re-enfranchising America's youngest generation of adults by eradicating student debt and pay the balance via savings no longer spent subsidizing illegal immigrants.

In his own words, regarding recent graduates: "They go, and they work, and they take loans, and they're borrowed up, and they can't breathe, and they get through college and the worst thing is, they go through that whole process and they don't have any job." Trump has it right. He sees how this rigged system has snuffed out the optimism of a bright generation that now gives way to cynicism and despair.

If I am elected as your Senator, I will help enact legislation that eradicates all Student Debt, effective immediately.

Boost Social Security Now

Social Security is no longer publicly discussed by our duplicitous media despite the fact that seniors' issues need the spotlight now more than ever. The media derided the implied greed of SSR recipients who received a whopping two percent cost of living raise to kick off 2018, as if oblivious to the fact that the inflation rate for 2017 was nearly 11%. Not 2%, but 11%.

No wonder seniors are struggling when their cost for purchases goes up 11% and their COLA to make up for that is a mere 2%. How do I know that, and you don't?

There are several ways Americans can investigate how much government lies cost them each year. The government purposely underestimates the cost of living to deprive our elderly of a commensurate actual increase in earned benefits. One such method for you to use is to subscribe to the Chapwood index or you may explore Shadowstats.com.

Seniors unfortunately are running out of whatever financial cushions they may ever have had, and their plight today is dire. I encourage you all to research the degree to which government deceptions are resulting in these surreptitious deprivations.

After decades being saturated by our mainstream propaganda rags, it is refreshing to finally see the truth in print. The Chapwood Index reflects the true cost-of-living increase in America. It is updated and released twice a year. There the ruses or mis-directions of the government are not included in its pages. Instead, it truthfully reports the unadjusted actual cost and price fluctuation of the top 500 items on which Americans spend their after-tax dollars in the 50 largest cities in the nation.

It exposes why middle-class Americans—salaried workers who are given routine pay hikes and retirees who depend on annual increases in their corporate pension and Social Security payments—cannot maintain their standard of living. Plainly and simply, the Index shows that their income can't keep up with their expenses and it explains why they increasingly have to turn to the government for entitlements for supplementation.

Mainstream Democrats like Senator Casey and Nancy Pelosi exacerbate the situation by allowing use of even more inequitable methods such as the new chained CPI to help assure that Seniors can languish in poverty as soon as possible.

The problem of lacking transparency on true costs (true inflation) occurs because salary and benefit increases are pegged to the fraudulent Consumer Price Index (CPI), which for more than a century has purported to reflect the fluctuation in prices for a typical "basket of goods" in American cities — but which actually hasn't done that for more than 30 years

The middle class has seen its purchasing power decline dramatically in the last three decades, forcing more and more people to seek entitlements when their savings are gone. And as long as pay raises and benefit increases are tied to a false CPI, this trend will continue.

In the past, nobody was anxious to throw the proverbial grandma under the bus. Now, believe it or not, hordes of constituencies are lining up to be the first to fleece what should belong to her into the eternal abyss, never to be seen again. The list of offenders includes: Congress, government officials, professors in academia, the "greatest" economic advisors the world has ever known, and dejected stand-alone economists who failed to gain tenure at a university.

This group of elite misfits have formed a diabolical consortium to cheat seniors out of their due cost of living increases promised from the very day the SSR act was passed by Franklin Delano Roosevelt.

As the mainstream Democrats kowtow to cultural elites and financial institutions, turning their backs on the workers and middle-class that defined their constituency for much of the 20th century, it is up to us to pick up the slack and fight for the rights of everyday Americans. When SSR was enacted, the president promised full dollar value throughout the years in order to ensure its passage in 1933. We cannot let this be undermined by the likes of Senator Casey and his allies under Chuck Schumer and Nancy Pelosi.

Many Americans are concerned that the Social Security program itself may not be able to sustain itself while others see the government cheating on the cost of living increases (CPI) thereby predetermining a life of squalor for seniors.

All successful societies throughout the ages, have maintained respect and dignity for their elders. Not only is cheating seniors a moral failure, it is a sign of a civilization entering an era of decay.

While seniors are losing their homes and many, for want of bread and milk, are on the verge of heading to the proverbial poorhouse or worse—the clutches of the Grim Reaper, Congress in 2018 pretended to care, giving a 2% raise, but then quickly snatched it right back in the dead of night via a Medicare Part B premium increase. This additional Medicare Part B charge for necessary health services for seniors was excluded from the cost of living calculations.

Thus, to pay Medicare part B, seniors are forced to use their "generous" 2% raises there, rather than to offset the costs brought forth from inflation in 2017 for which the 2% was intended. Since the real inflationary cost increases were closer to 11%, that means that instead of 9% that seniors were to endure, they accrued a full load of 11% in price increases. It's easy to understand why this constant drainage of resources is unsustainable for a senior citizen.

How did we reach this point?

Early in the administration of disgraced former President Bill Clinton, an economist named Michael Boskin, and Alan Greenspan, Chairman of the Board of Governors of the Federal Reserve System, devised a scheme that would allow for market basket "substitutions" to artificially lower the cost of living and result in lower payments to our oldest Americans. Prior to their involvement, the consumer price index (CPI) was measured using the cost of a fixed basket of goods, a fairly simple and straightforward concept.

The identical basket of goods would be priced at prevailing market costs for each period, and the period-to-period change in the cost of that market basket represented the rate of inflation in terms of maintaining a constant standard of living. That was self-evidently fair and reasonable, and predictably resulted in seniors receiving annual COLA increases in tandem with the prices of goods actually increasing.

But Boskin and Alan Greenspan argued that when one item in the basket, for instance steak, became too expensive, the consumer would substitute hamburger for the steak, and that the inflation measure should reflect the costs tied to buying hamburger rather than the steak. Eventually, it became OK for the bureaucrats to replace hamburger with less expensive tuna and eventually because the protein value was the same, cat tuna replaced regular tuna in the market basket.

To further obscure the true cost of living, other items were selectively removed from the basket when the prices were high and then reinserted when the prices were low.

Many people have been familiar with this ruse. For example, a 1970s economic commentator named Barry Ritholtz joked that Greenspan's core inflation metric can more accurately be described as "inflation ex-inflation," meaning inflation after all of the inflation has been excluded. This demonstrates that the deception of seniors has been intentional, and it continues with a new notion called the chained CPI that will cost seniors even more.

The fact is that government has deceitfully stolen right from the pockets of our beloved seniors by denying them a fair cost of living increase. Some have even suggested that the government believes a natural limit exists on the criticism this could engender because over time, many of the complaints will be silenced by their deaths. Charming.

Walter J. Williams, an American blessing who operates the Shadowstats site has demonstrated that seniors have been stiffed by much more than just 125% and in fact should be receiving more than 4 times what their dollars were worth in 1980. That's $450 instead of $100.00. Any senior would love to have even a small proportion of that loss back.

I hope I have convinced you all that seniors have been ripped off and are being ripped off financially by their government. Congress is the real culprit.

So, what do I recommend for now? A gradual remedy. Since it would be difficult to give seniors the proper increase immediately needed to offset this quagmire caused by government malfeasance, my recommendation would be to approach it gradually, in a way that seniors would be somewhat pleased, and be able to live out their golden years in a more dignified manner.

For the next four years, the COLA boost that I'd recommend would be 15% above the real inflation rate. After four consecutive years, that should be sufficient to remove seniors from the on-deck circle they currently occupy directly outside the homeless shelter. That's all it would take.

Thank you for your attention on these important matters.

In conclusion, I must again express my gratitude for your consideration and any support as we work together to make America even greater.

God bless America and help us all make her better!

Other Books by Brian Kelly: (amazon.com, and Kindle)

It's Time for The John Doe Party… Don't you think? By By Elephants.
Great Players in Florida Gators Football… Tim Tebow and a ton of other great players
Great Coaches in Florida Gators Football… The best coaches in Gator history.
The Constitution by Hamilton, Jefferson, Madison, et al. The Real Constitution
The Constitution Companion. Will help you learn and understand the Constitution
Great Coaches in Clemson Football The best Clemson Coaches right to Dabo Sinney
Great Players in Clemson Football The best Clemson players in history
Winning Back America. America's been stolen and can be won back completely
The Founding of America… Great book to pick up a lot of great facts
Defeating America's Career Politicians. The scoundrels need to go.
Midnight Mass by Jack Lammers… You remember what it was like Hreat story
The Bike by Jack Lammers… Great heartwarming Story by Jack
Wipe Out All Student Loan Debt--Now! Watch the economy go boom!
No Free Lunch Pay Back Welfare! Why not pay it back?
Deport All Millennials Now!!! Why they deserve to be deported and/or saved
DELETE the EPA, Please! The worst decisions to hurt America
Taxation Without Representation 4th Edition Should we throw the TEA overboard again?
Four Great Political Essays by Thomas Dawson
Top Ten Political Books for 2018… Cliffnotes Version of 10 Political Books
Top Six Patriotic Books for 2018… Cliffnotes version of 6 Patriotic Boosk
Why Trump Got Elected!.. It's great to hear about a great milestone in America!
The Day the Free Press Died. Corrupt Press Lives on!
Solved (Immigration) The best solutions for 2018
Solved II (Obamacare, Social Security, Student Debt) Check it out; They're solved.
Great Moments in Pittsburgh Steelers Football... Six Super Bowls and more.
Great Players in Pittsburgh Steelers Football ,,,Chuck Noll, Bill Cowher, Mike Tomin, etc.
Great Coaches in New England Patriots Football,,, Bill Belichick the one and only plus others
Great Players in New England Patriots Football… Tom Brady, Drew Bledsoe et al.
Great Coaches in Philadelphia Eagles Football..Andy Reid, Doug Pederson & Lots more
Great Players in Philadelphia Eagles Football Great players such as Sonny Jurgenson
Great Coaches in Syracuse Football All the greats including Ben Schwartzwalder
Great Players in Syracuse Football. Highlights best players such as Jim Brown & Donovan McNabb
Millennials are People Too !!! Give US millennials help to live American Dream
Brian Kelly for the United States Senate from PA: Fresh Face for US Senate
The Candidate's Bible. Don't pray for your campaign without this bible
Rush Limbaugh's Platform for Americans… Rush will love it
Sean Hannity's Platform for Americans… Sean will love it
Donald Trump's New Platform for Americans. Make Trump unbeatable in 2020
Tariffs Are Good for America! One of the best tools a president can have
Great Coaches in Pittsburgh Steelers Football Sixteen of the best coaches ever to coach in pro football.
Great Moments in New England Patriots Football Great football moments from Boston to New England
Great Moments in Philadelphia Eagles Football. The best from the Eagles from the beginning of football.
Great Moments in Syracuse Football The great moments, coaches & players in Syracuse Football
Boost Social Security Now! Hey Buddy Can You Spare a Dime?
The Birth of American Football. From the first college game in 1869 to the last Super Bowl
Obamacare: A One-Line Repeal Congress must get this done.
A Wilkes-Barre Christmas Story A wonderful town makes Christmas all the better
A Boy, A Bike, A Train, and a Christmas Miracle A Christmas story that will melt your heart
Pay-to-Go   America-First Immigration Fix
Legalizing Illegal Aliens Via Resident Visas Americans-first plan saves $Trillions. Learn how!
60 Million Illegal Aliens in America!!! A simple, America-first solution.
The Bill of Rights By Founder James Madison Refresh *your knowledge of the specific rights for all*
Great Players in Army Football Great Army Football played by great players..
Great Coaches in Army Football Army's coaches are all great.
Great Moments in Army Football Army Football at its best.
Great Moments in Florida Gators Football Gators Football from the start. This is the book.
Great Moments in Clemson Football CU Football at its best. This is the book.
Great Moments in Florida Gators Football Gators Football from the start. This is the book.
The Constitution Companion. A Guide to Reading and Comprehending the Constitution
The Constitution by Hamilton, Jefferson, & Madison – Big type and in English

PATERNO: The Dark Days After Win # 409. Sky began to fall within days of win # 409.
JoePa 409 Victories: Say No More! Winningest Division I-A football coach ever
American College Football: The Beginning From before day one football was played.
Great Coaches in Alabama Football Challenging the coaches of every other program!
Great Coaches in Penn State Football the Best Coaches in PSU's football program
Great Players in Penn State Football The best players in PSU's football program
Great Players in Notre Dame Football The best players in ND's football program
Great Coaches in Notre Dame Football The best coaches in any football program
Great Players in Alabama Football from Quarterbacks to offensive Linemen Greats!
Great Moments in Alabama Football AU Football from the start. This is the book.
Great Moments in Penn State Football PSU Football, start--games, coaches, players,
Great Moments in Notre Dame Football ND Football, start, games, coaches, players
Cross Country with the Parents A great trip from East Coast to West with the kids
Seniors, Social Security & the Minimum Wage. Things seniors need to know.
How to Write Your First Book and Publish It with CreateSpace
The US Immigration Fix--It's all in here. Finally, an answer.
I had a Dream IBM Could be #1 Again The title is self-explanatory
WineDiets.Com Presents The Wine Diet Learn how to lose weight while having fun.
Wilkes-Barre, PA; Return to Glory Wilkes-Barre City's return to glory
Geoffrey Parsons' Epoch... The Land of Fair Play Better than the original.
The Bill of Rights 4 Dummmies! This is the best book to learn about your rights.
Sol Bloom's Epoch ...Story of the Constitution The best book to learn the Constitution
America 4 Dummmies! All Americans should read to learn about this great country.
The Electoral College 4 Dummmies! How does it really work?
The All-Everything Machine Story about IBM's finest computer server.
ThankYou IBM! This book explains how IBM was beaten in the computer marketplace by neophytes

Brian has written 171 books in total. Other books can be found at
amazon.com/author/brianwkelly